Motivating Hard to Reach Students

Motivating Hard to Reach Students

by Barbara L. McCombs and James E. Pope

AMERICAN PSYCHOLOGICAL ASSOCIATION | WASHINGTON, DC

Published by
American Psychological Association
750 First Street, NE
Washington, DC 20002

Copies may be ordered from
APA Order Department
P.O. Box 2710
Hyattsville, MD 20784

In the UK and Europe, copies may be ordered from
American Psychological Association
3 Henrietta Street
Covent Garden, London
WC2E 8LU England

Typeset in Berkeley and Arbitrary Sans by KINETIK Communication Graphics, Inc., Washington, DC

Printer: Data Reproductions Corp., Rochester Hills, MI
Cover Designer: KINETIK Communication Graphics, Inc., Washington, DC
Technical/Production Editor: Paula R. Bronstein

Library of Congress Cataloging-in-Publication Data
McCombs, Barbara L.
    Motivating hard to reach students / by Barbara L. McCombs and James E. Pope.
      p.   cm. — (Psychology in the classroom: a series on applied educational psychology)
      ISBN 1-55798-220-1 (acid-free paper)
      1. Motivation in education. 2. Motivation in education—Case studies. I. Pope, James E. II. Title. III. Series: Psychology in the classroom.
LB1065.M346 1994
370.15'4—dc20   94-8336
                                            CIP

British Library Cataloguing-in-Publication Data
A CIP record is available from the British Library.

Printed in the United States of America
First Edition

TABLE OF CONTENTS

PREFACE

Trying to reach students who have lost interest in learning and have lost the motivation to learn, or students who are defeated or turned off to school for any number of reasons, is a frustrating and all too common experience for teachers in today's classrooms and schools. This booklet was written in order to share our ideas with you, the elementary, middle school, and high school teacher. It presents our own perspective on and approach to motivating hard to reach students. We believe that this look at what we know about motivation and the strategies we suggest will be valuable to you personally as well as to your students.

The information in this book is based on the assumption that all students are motivated to learn under the right conditions, and that you can provide these conditions in your classroom. Although we recognize that providing these conditions is far easier with the support and encouragement of your administrative staff, even without this support there are things you can do to empower both yourself and your students. In this book, we have assembled many practical strategies and activities that you can tailor to meet your own and your students' needs.

We have seen this approach work, and we are excited about its possibilities. We invite you to explore this perspective with us.

Finally, this book is designed to be more than just a discussion of how to motivate hard to reach students. It is an interactive workbook designed to help you devise new ways of reaching even the most unmotivated students. We invite you to become actively involved in reflecting on what the insights and tools mean to you by thoughtfully responding to the questions at the end of each section. We also urge you to adapt and photocopy any of the exercises for use with your students.

introduction

In your experience as a teacher you have probably had occasion to deal with problems similar to the two cases presented below. Note the way you would handle each situation, given your present philosophy on how to motivate students. This will give you a baseline for understanding the way your thoughts and strategies might change as a result of working through this book.

STUDENT CASE ILLUSTRATION: SASHA

Sasha is a second-grade student in a large, inner-city elementary school. She had been excited about going to school when she started first grade, but the year did not go well for her. Some of the other students in her class already knew how to read when they started school, and by the end of first grade, they were in advanced reading groups. Other students who were able to do pretty well with reading were in the regular reading group, but Sasha and a few other children who had difficulty with reading ended up in the low group. Now that she is in second grade, Sasha is even further behind and she hates being in the low group. She feels so dumb when she has trouble reading in class, and the other kids laugh at her. Her teacher is becoming impatient and frustrated because of Sasha's increasingly sullen attitude. As a result, Sasha has become even more withdrawn and unwilling to try. Her teacher has contacted Sasha's mother to try to arrange some special tutoring in reading. Although Sasha's mother wants to help, she is clearly overwhelmed by her five other children, with no father around and extremely limited finances. Sasha's teacher has no idea what to do next. She knows Sasha could learn to read and achieve well with the right help and motivation.

SELF-DIRECTED QUESTION

☐ What would you do if you were Sasha's teacher?

STUDENT CASE ILLUSTRATION: DERRIN

Derrin is an eighth-grade student at a small urban middle school. He enrolled in the school in October but withdrew before December. In February of the same school year, he re-enrolled in the school. He attends school very sporadically, usually only two or three days a week. His teachers have been quite frustrated with Derrin. Although he seems very bright and scores above average on many tests and projects, his poor attendance and failure to complete most work keeps his grades at an F level. He has missed many classes due to referrals and suspensions received for behavioral outbursts. Derrin's main interest is heavy metal rock groups. In fact, his teachers are impressed with his ability to name all the members of most heavy metal bands. His interest is reflected in his dress and manner, which are unusual for this school because there are relatively few students with similar interests. As a result, he has formed very few friendships and spends a good part of his day by himself. Efforts to contact his parents have been fruitless. Derrin is apparently living temporarily with an uncle in the neighborhood. The uncle says he has little influence over Derrin's activities and that Derrin spends very few nights at home. His teachers know he has the ability to be a high achiever, but they are frustrated by his poor attendance and behavior patterns.

What would you do if you were Derrin's teacher?

Although the students in the two preceding examples are very different, they share a common problem. They have developed negative attitudes about themselves and school, and consequently have lost touch with their motivation to learn.

Unfortunately, these types of students are becoming increasingly common in the nation's schools, from elementary through secondary school levels and beyond. Because of this rising problem and its correlates (e.g., attrition, delinquency, and drug use), teachers are increasingly feeling the need to know more about how to motivate hard to reach students and how to encourage students to have positive attitudes toward themselves and toward learning. In addition, teachers often feel powerless to deal with the complex problems students bring with them to the classroom.

That's what this book is all about: providing you with some principles and practical methods for stimulating motivation in students who have lost touch with their natural desire to learn. The information and strategies are also designed to empower you, as well as your students, by helping you to understand motivation and how it can be enhanced in even the most hard to reach students at the elementary, middle school, and high school levels.

The examples provided illustrate the kinds of activities that can be used with various age groups at these levels of schooling. They are not intended as "cookbook" procedures that can be instantly applied to the teaching situation, but rather are intended as idea sources. We know that the cookbook approach is less effective than approaches that focus on genuine respect for students and an understanding of their innate potential and their motivation to learn. Furthermore, there could never be enough "recipes" for dealing with the unique students, their needs, and the situations you will encounter in your classrooms. The goal is for you to trust your creativity and be guided by the activities and principles provided here.

This book has been designed both for self-study and for use in graduate-level education classes or continuing education workshops. We have provided self-directed questions, with write-in space, to help you review the principles presented, as well as self-directed activities to help you devise activities that you can use in your own classroom.

The book starts with a brief overview of current research and theory on motivation. In this overview we have summarized what we consider to be the most important findings on the topic. At the end of the section, we have provided a list of suggested readings, all by authors mentioned, for those of you who wish to read more on the theories of motivation. Next, we look at what these current views mean for your role as teacher. The suggested readings listed at the end of this section are more practice-oriented. We then move on to present specific strategies and activities that you can use to enhance motivation in students and to create the kind of classroom in which positive changes can take place.

Before we begin, let's look at what we hope you will learn from this book:

STATEMENT OF RATIONALE AND GOALS

Rationale

An understanding of student motivation, and how it can be supported and encouraged, can help you experience a more rewarding teaching career. This understanding can also help you contribute to more positive student growth and development, thereby reducing problems like student failure and attrition.

Goals

1. To help you understand the nature of motivation and how it can be enhanced.

2. To help you understand what impact the nature of motivation may have on your overall role as a teacher.

3. To provide you with some strategies for helping individual students draw on their natural motivation to learn.

4. To provide you with some strategies for establishing a classroom climate that fosters and sustains motivation.

goal one

Understanding the Nature
of Motivation

Teachers recognize that motivation is important for learning and therefore want to have motivated students. Over the years, they have used a variety of approaches to motivate students with problems similar to those of the students you met in our introductory examples, Sasha and Derrin. Rarely, however, do they receive training on how to motivate students. And when training is provided, it usually stresses techniques that do not capitalize on the vast amount of research on motivation and exciting new approaches based on this research. Thus, teachers have had to rely on commonsense approaches that are based on their teaching experiences, independent study of suggestions from research, intuition, training in particular techniques, consultations with other teachers, or any combination of these approaches.

The frustrations that many teachers feel in trying to motivate hard to reach students come from the realities of time pressure, the high number of students with learning and emotional needs, heavy accountability demands from administrators and parents, and other stress-producing situations that exist in many of our schools. Attempts to rely on outdated training and intuition often fall short in the heat of a difficult situation with a student. Similar to situations in parenting, just when we most need to recall that specific technique we learned for positively disciplining or getting the attention of a child, time pressures and our own stress level prevent us from remembering what it was we were supposed to do. In the case of teaching, this often results in attempts to keep the classroom quiet and well-disciplined rather than attempts to enhance students' motivation to learn.

When you think about it, almost everything you do in the classroom has a motivational influence on students, including the way you present information, the kinds of exercises you use, the way you interact with students, and the opportunities you give students to work alone or in groups. Students react to who you are, what you do, and how comfortable they feel in your classroom. In spite of this enormous motivational influence, teachers have few tools for understanding motivation and how to enhance it in their students.

We've found that it's helpful for teachers to see what those studying motivation are discovering about the nature of motivation to learn and the ways motivation can be developed or enhanced in students. In this section, we will provide you with a concise review of the literature on motivation from our perspective. With this information, you can evaluate whether the theories and suggested strategies might be helpful from your perspective. It is our intent to provide you with an opportunity to review and reflect on what we see as some exciting theories on the nature of motivation to learn. As you read, we invite you to think about Sasha and Derrin, your current strategies for motivating students, and the implications of the perspectives presented here for new approaches and strategies.

CURRENT THEORIES OF MOTIVATION

Psychologists studying human behavior have proposed many different theories of motivation. Early on, Sigmund Freud proposed that humans start out with certain basic biological drives or instincts that motivate individuals to behave in certain ways. The job of educators was viewed as helping students control and direct these drives. Later, behaviorists, such as B.F. Skinner, proposed that humans start out in life with a blank slate on which experiences and external events gradually condition certain behavior. According to the behaviorist theory, motivation and learning could be controlled by managing behavior through external rewards and incentives such as tokens, prizes, or even grades. Humanistic psychologists, such as Abraham Maslow and Carl Rogers, proposed that individuals begin life with a propensity for growth or self-actualization, but that learning, natural development, and significant others or events facilitate this process. Motivation was seen largely as the unfolding of certain basic needs or tendencies that were supported or hindered by the environment.

In the past 25 years, cognitive, social–cognitive, and social–behaviorist perspectives have arisen to extend and refine these earlier theories. The cognitive perspective focuses on the study of mental processes and emphasizes the importance of perception in learning and memory, along with the importance of the active role of the student and the recognition that all knowledge is personal knowledge constructed from each individual's unique belief system and frame of reference. Within most current cognitive theories, however, the major focus has been on how the mind structures and organizes experience. From this perspective, motivation is based on an individual's learned beliefs about his or her worth, abilities, or competencies (e.g., academic self-concepts); goals and expectations for success or failure; and the positive or negative feelings (e.g., curiosity, anxiety) that result from self-evaluative processes. Research by Albert Bandura, Marty Covington, Carol Dweck, Jackie Eccles, Susan Harter, Hazel Markus, Bernie Weiner, and others working in this area has helped us understand that learned self-beliefs, goals, expectations, and feelings influence motivation and performance.

Both internal and external factors play important roles in defining the nature of motivation and how to enhance its effect.

Another set of theories from a social–cognitive or social–behaviorist perspective emphasizes the importance of external factors in motivation to learn, including social and emotional support from significant others (e.g., genuine caring, respect, and encouragement) and external rewards and incentives in the environment (e.g., being recognized for accomplishments). Because of the complexity of motivation, people disagree about the relative importance of internal factors (beliefs) and external factors (rewards) for motivation, and a number of theories of intrinsic (internal) versus extrinsic (external) motivation have been posited. In spite of these disagreements, we are beginning to see consensus on and integration of competing theories in several important areas; such a consensus may help define the nature of motivation and how best to enhance it during learning. For example, work on intrinsic motivation by Margaret Clifford, Ed Deci, John Nicholls, and others has helped us understand that individuals have a natural tendency to be intrinsically motivated when they focus on personal learning goals. The research also shows that individuals are naturally motivated to learn when they do not have to fear failure, when they perceive what they are learning as being personally meaningful and relevant, and when they are in supportive and respectful relationships with teachers. In addition, research by James Connell, Richard Ryan, and others has shown the importance of supporting students' needs for autonomy or self-determination. That is, their research shows that students are more motivated to learn when teachers provide them with opportunities to make decisions and to have some control over the learning process.

Recent theories of motivation are also beginning to focus on higher level processes (such as *metacognition* or the ability to think about one's own thinking) and on how we can engage higher levels of self-awareness, or consciousness, in order to control our thinking. When individuals learn that they can operate outside the cognitive or learned system of beliefs, they experience a deep sense of personal control. The focus in this research is on an understanding of the self as agent. In our own research with both teachers and students, we have found that learned knowledge and beliefs about the self (such as a self-concept that "I am not good at math") will play a primary role in motivation and behavior only if individuals are not aware that they can choose how to interpret the influence or control that these thoughts and beliefs have on their feelings and behavior. Psychologists Rick Suarez, Roger Mills, and Darlene Stewart argue that if individuals do not recognize the choice to selectively use their thought system, they operate unconsciously within the limits of that thought system; that is, they are controlled by rather than in control of their beliefs and thoughts. When individuals can be taught to understand and control their thinking, they can step outside the influence of negative beliefs about their abilities or fear of failure. As a result, they can access higher level processes such as insight, creativity, wisdom, and common sense. They can operate outside the cognitive system and see beyond a conditioned belief system or personal frame of reference.

> Individuals are often unaware of their role in constructing personal realities.

In a nutshell, what is emerging as a new perspective relating to motivation is that students are capable of understanding the relationships between their beliefs, their feelings, and their motivation. At higher levels of understanding or consciousness, students can see that they have personal control (or agency) over thought content and thinking processes, they can understand the role of thought, and they can know that they have the ability to be self-motivated. Psychologist Rick Suarez argues that it is the function of thought that provides a more primary level of agency than the content of thought (e.g., beliefs, values, expectancies, and goals). Thought is the immediate cause of all beliefs, and it can be controlled consciously and voluntarily. Because thinking is such a habit, we are not aware of it and many times do not view ourselves as having an active role in constructing our own personal realities or belief systems. Increasing an individual's awareness of being actively engaged at any moment in creating thoughts, beliefs, or attitudes is the first step in helping that individual perceive his or her control over the creation of personal realities. Roger Mills believes that if individuals understand thought as a function, they are empowered by experiencing voluntary control of their thinking and, in turn, their emotions, motivation, and behavior.

> Understanding the function of thought helps individuals voluntarily control their thoughts, emotions, motivation, and behavior.

These recent views of motivation, then, help us understand that the content of thought (e.g., beliefs, and goals) causes motivation only to the degree that individuals are unaware of their role as agent in constructing and directing thoughts, that is, in choosing the level of influence specific beliefs will have in a given situation. At higher levels of understanding, individuals can override the influence or their beliefs through their choice of thoughts. Furthermore, in the view of Ed Deci and Richard Ryan, agency is an inherent tendency of the self to originate

> Motivation is an inherent, natural capacity to learn in positive ways; it needs to be elicited rather than established.

behavior, to relate to and assimilate events, and to gain a sense of personal control and competence; it is the basis for self-determination or actions that result from the perception of self as agent. At the core, the self is said to have an energizing component termed *intrinsic* or *growth motivation*. The true self is characterized as operating when one's actions are endorsed by oneself with integrity and with a view of oneself as the locus of active development. Thus, motivation, from the perspective of research reviewed here, can be understood as a natural capacity and tendency within the person to learn and grow in positive ways. Because motivation is inherent, it needs to be elicited rather than established.

WHAT DOES RESEARCH IMPLY ABOUT PRINCIPLES OF EFFECTIVE PRACTICE?

The research in the previous section implies that for students to be able to draw on their inherent motivation to learn, they must understand the ways their thinking can influence their moods and behavior. They need to understand the concept of self as agent and what it means. For example, if a student has negative beliefs (e.g., "I don't have the ability to succeed in math"), these beliefs can be overridden by an understanding that "I can control the thoughts (and hence, the emotions) that feed those beliefs. Even if I perceive that certain background or ability factors can interfere with my success, I recognize that it is my thoughts about these factors that will interfere with positive feelings and motivation to learn. Therefore, I can choose to redirect my thoughts, gain a different perspective, and work to overcome these barriers with effort and training in skill enhancing strategies that can offset these negative influences."

> The potential for positive functioning exists for all students, at-risk or not.

Helping students with those choices that lead to healthier thoughts, feelings, and motivation requires more than skill training and a redesigned curriculum. What is particularly essential is that students be in instructional environments that provide genuine caring and support from teachers, classmates, and other people in the system. This environment needs to include instructional practices (e.g., direct instruction in thinking skills, cooperative learning groups, or other opportunities for independent thought and problem solving) that give students real experience in how to use their minds and how to take personal control over their thought processes. When students can be helped to understand, through personal and instructional supports, how their minds work and how to control their thought processes, their natural capacities for higher level thinking and motivation to learn can be elicited. Self-regulation can become a self-confirming cycle, and a positive spiral of higher level understanding and functioning can result.

> Successful programs foster enhanced interpersonal relationships that create an optimal climate for learning.

Some of our own recent work on motivational interventions for high-risk youth has resulted in a Reciprocal Empowerment Model.[1] The model explains the principles of motivation that operate for all individuals in an educational system. It builds on work by both Roger Mills and Richard Ryan and assumes that within all individuals, whether at-risk or not, there is a core of mental health (a potential for positive functioning that includes natural self-esteem and motivation to learn). Their research has shown that when young people are in positive relationships with others and are taught about their own thought processes, they become eager to learn. Thus, the model is one that focuses on promoting the mental health, motivation, and potential of youth through addressing will, skill, and social support training components.

> The development of positive belief systems by students and teachers is reciprocal.

Within the Reciprocal Empowerment Model, *will* is defined as an innate or self-actualized state of motivation, an internal state of well-being, in which individuals are in touch with their natural self-esteem, common sense, and intrinsic motivation to learn. *Skill* is defined as an acquired cognitive or metacognitive competency (such

[1]McCombs, B. L. & Marzano, R. J. (1990). Putting the self in self-regulated learning: The self as agent in integrating will and skill. *Educational Psychologist, 25*(1), 51-69.

as becoming more aware of one's control over thinking) that develops with training or practice. *Social support* is the interpersonal context that enables the empowerment of will and the development of skill components, specifically through quality relationships and interactions with others.

The term *reciprocal* is used in this model to mean that students can only be empowered (i.e., feel competent and in control) to the degree that those around them provide positive support and quality relationships. In order for parents, teachers, and other significant people in students' lives to provide these positive teaching and learning experiences in genuinely respectful and caring ways, they themselves must feel competent and in control. For example, teachers need to feel the respect and support of their administrative staff in order to exercise the creativity and flexibility necessary to work with students in meaningful ways. Thus, common principles of empowerment work reciprocally for all individuals in the system.

> Successful programs are centered around quality relationships between adults and youth.

RESEARCH ON WHAT WORKS WITH HARD TO MOTIVATE STUDENTS

In separate reviews of drug abuse and dropout prevention interventions undertaken for the National Institute of Drug Abuse (NIDA) and the U.S. Department of Education, Roger Mills and Nancy Peck (with collaborators, Annmarie Law and Roger Mills)[2] discovered that the program elements that clearly contributed to program success were relatively simple and straightforward. The most important common element of successful programs was the quality of the relationships established between adults and youth. Successful relationships stemmed from a genuine caring for students and an understanding of the optimal climate for learning. Thus, it seems to matter less what is done than who does it and how. As Peck and her colleagues state,

[2]Mills, R.C. (1990, June). Substance abuse, dropout, and delinquency prevention: An innovative approach. Paper presented at the 8th annual conference of the Psychology of Mind, St. Petersburg, Florida.

Peck, N., Law, A., & Mills, R.C. (1989). Dropout prevention: What we have learned. Ann Arbor, MI: ERIC Counseling and Personnel Services Clearinghouse.

All research concludes that at-risk youth have poorer self-concepts than other students, higher insecurity about their ability to fit in at school, and higher subjective perceptions that school is not for them. Staff must be the kind of people who are not only committed to, but optimistic about, reaching these youth. They must also be the kind of people who are able to bypass this insecure frame of reference and reach students at a deeper level of mental health, motivation, and common sense.

Many programs for high-risk youth are not having the necessary impact because they assume there is something to be fixed or something that is missing in these youth. Roger Mills and others question this assumption because it inadvertently serves to support a negative mindset in youth. A mindset consists of beliefs and attitudes individuals hold regarding themselves, others, and reality, through which they perceive and interpret experiences. A negative mindset prevents young people from achieving healthier levels of functioning that can be brought out from within and nurtured. Mills' work demonstrates that negative ways of performing and reacting are the product of learned insecure thinking that has obscured youths' natural common sense, ability to learn by insight, and feelings of well-being. Many hard to reach youth are from unhealthy families or cultures in which they have developed insecure belief systems. Combined with negative school and community experiences, this results in increasing feelings of alienation and isolation from normal peers and lifestyles. A majority of high-risk youth are chronically in low mood states and perceive things in negatively biased ways. This combination of insecure perceptions, feelings, and behaviors leads to problems like school failure, attrition, and delinquency.

> Insecure beliefs, feelings, and behaviors cover up natural motivation, but can be bypassed by quality relationships.

SUMMARY

We have briefly covered current theories of motivation and discussed how these theories have changed in recent years. Today's theories of motivation focus more on what individuals think about themselves and their abilities to learn rather than on their behaviors. In addition, current theories stress that motivation to learn is a natural capacity that exists in all students when they are in positive states of mind and have a supportive learning environment. Even students who look as though they have lost their motivation to learn can regain this natural capacity and grow in positive ways.

The challenge for you, as a teacher, is to reach these hard to motivate students. You need to find ways to get past negative thoughts, feelings, and behavior and reach the inherent health and motivation. You need to help students see this health and regain their motivation to learn. It is how to accomplish this in your classroom that is the topic of the remainder of this booklet.

At the end of Goal 1 is a list of suggested readings that will help you understand the nature of motivation.

1 Based on your reading of the research and theory discussed in this section, what do you think are some general principles that may be applied when working to motivate hard to reach students?

2 Describe how these principles reinforce what you already know about teaching hard to motivate students.

3 Have the principles described here changed your view of the factors that motivate hard to reach students? How?

4 Has your understanding of these concepts changed your response to the examples of Sasha and Derrin? How?

5 Describe a hard to reach student you have taught in the past. What were his or her behavior characteristics? How did these characteristics impact his or her school performance? Have the concepts described changed your views regarding the ways you would work with this student? How?

ANSWERS TO QUESTIONS

1 Some general principles you may have thought of that apply to motivating hard to reach students include:

a. An individual's motivation is based on that person's previously learned beliefs regarding his or her worth and abilities. An individual will establish expectations of success or failure and will develop either positive or negative feelings based on learned beliefs.

b. Internal and external factors both play important roles in determining the nature of student motivation.

c. At higher levels of thought, students have the ability to understand the relationship between their system of beliefs and their natural tendency to be self-motivated.

d. Individuals are often unaware of their role in constructing personal realities.

e. Because motivation is inherent (i.e., a part of the naturally existing core of positive mental health), it must be elicited, not established.

2 Although we are not sure of your current level of knowledge, most teachers generally understand the role that teacher expectations play in student achievement. The idea that all students, hard to motivate or not, have a natural motivation to learn, is also commonly held. What may be new is the principle that the core of positive mental health can be readily accessed by teachers when they understand the nature of motivation and have the skills needed to provide a supportive and caring learning environment.

3 Answers will vary.

4 Answers will vary; however, there should be some indication that an effective approach to motivating Sasha and Derrin will involve placing more emphasis on establishing a quality relationship between student and teacher. The research perspective presented here suggests that if a positive and optimal climate for learning is developed, the student's natural tendency to be self-motivated will be elicited.

5 Answers will vary.

SUGGESTED READINGS

Bandura, A. (1989). Human agency in social cognitive theory. *American Psychologist, 44*(9), 1175–1184.

Bandura, A. (1991). Self-regulation of motivation through anticipatory and self-reactive mechanisms. In R. Dienstbier (Ed.), *Nebraska symposium on motivation: Vol. 38. Perspectives on motivation* (Vol. 38, pp. 69–164). Lincoln: University of Nebraska Press.

Clifford, M. M. (1984). Thoughts on a theory of constructive failure. *Educational Psychologist, 19*(2), 108–120.

Connell, J. P., & Wellborn, J. G. (1991). Competence, autonomy, and relatedness: A motivational analysis of self-system processes. In M. Gunnar & L. A. Sroufe (Eds.), *Minnesota symposium on child psychology* (Vol. 23, pp. 43–77). Hillsdale, NJ: Erlbaum.

Covington, M. V. (1985). The motive for self-worth. In C. Ames & R. Ames (Eds.), *Research on motivation in education: The classroom milieu* (pp. 77–113). San Diego, CA: Academic Press.

Deci, E. L. (1980). *The psychology of self-determination.* Lexington, MA: Heath.

Deci, E. L., & Ryan, R. M. (1985). *Intrinsic motivation and self-determination in human behavior.* New York: Plenum Press.

Deci, E. L., & Ryan, R. M. (1991). A motivational approach to self: Integration in personality. In R. Dienstbier (Ed.), *Nebraska symposium on motivation: Vol. 38.* Perspectives on motivation (pp. 237–288). Lincoln: University of Nebraska Press.

Dweck, C. S. (1986). Motivational processes affecting learning. *American Psychologist, 41*, 1040–1048.

Dweck, C. S. (1991). Self-theories and goals: Their role in motivation, personality, and development. In R. Dienstbier (Ed.), *Nebraska symposium on motivation: Vol. 38*. Perspectives on motivation. Lincoln: University of Nebraska Press.

Dweck, C. S., & Leggett, E. L. (1988). A social–cognitive approach to motivation and personality. *Psychological Review*, 95, 256–273.

Eccles, J. (1983). Expectancies, values, and academic behaviors. In J. Spence (Ed.), *Achievement and achievement motives: Psychological and sociological approaches* (pp. 75–146). San Francisco: Freeman.

Harter, S. (1986). Processes underlying self-concept formation in children. In J. H. Suls & A. Greenwald (Eds.), *Psychological perspectives on the self* (Vol. 3, pp. 137–181). Hillsdale, NJ: Erlbaum.

Harter, S. (1988). The construction and conservation of the self: James and Cooley revisited. In D. K. Lapsley & F. C. Power (Eds.), *Self, ego, and identity: Integrative approaches* (pp. 43–70). New York: Springer-Verlag.

Markus, H. M., & Nurius, P. (1987). Possible selves: The interface between motivation and the self-concept. In K. Yardley & T. Honess (Eds.), *Self and identity: Psychosocial perspectives* (pp. 157–172). New York: Wiley.

Markus, H. M., & Ruvulo, A. (1990). Possible selves: Personalized representations of goals. In L. Pervin (Ed.), *Goal concepts in psychology* (pp. 211–241). Hillsdale, NJ: Erlbaum.

McCombs, B. L. (1986). The role of the self-system in self-regulated learning. *Contemporary Educational Psychology*, 11, 314–332.

McCombs, B. L. (1989). Self-regulated learning and academic achievement: A phenomenological view. In B. J. Zimmerman & D. H. Schunk (Eds.), *Self-regulated learning and academic achievement: Theory, research, and practice* (pp. 51–82). New York: Springer-Verlag.

McCombs, B. L., & Marzano, R. J. (1990). Putting the self in self-regulated learning: The self as agent in integrating will and skill. *Educational Psychologist*, 25(1), 51–69.

Nicholls, J. G. (1983). Conceptions of ability and achievement motivation: A theory and its implications for education. In S. G. Paris, G. M. Olson, & H. W. Stevenson (Eds.), *Learning and motivation in the classroom* (pp. 211–237). Hillsdale, NJ: Erlbaum.

Nicholls, J. G. (1984). Achievement motivation: Conceptions of ability, subjective experience, task choice, and performance. *Psychological Review*, 91(3), 328–346.

Ryan, R. M. (1993). The nature of the self in autonomy and relatedness. In G. R. Goethals & J. Strauss (Eds.), *Multidisciplinary perspectives on the self* (pp. 208–238). New York: Springer-Verlag.

Ryan, R. M., & Stiller, J. (1991). The social contexts of internalization: Parent and teacher influences on autonomy, motivation, and learning. In M. L. Maehr & P. R. Pintrich (Eds.), *Advances in motivation and achievement* (Vol. 7, pp. 115–149). Greenwich, CT: JAI Press.

Suarez, E. M. (1988). A neo-cognitive dimension. *The Counseling Psychologist*, 16(2), 239–244.

Suarez, R., Mills, R. C., & Stewart, D. (1987). *Sanity, insanity, and common sense.* New York: Fawcett Columbine.

Weiner, B. (1990). History of motivational research in education. *Journal of Educational Psychology.* 82(4), 616–622.

goal two

Understanding Motivation
and How It Can Be Enhanced

In the past, most of the emphasis was placed on the role of teaching, that is, of helping students acquire and remember information in a variety of content areas. In the teaching role, teachers have primarily been concerned with how to present facts, examples, or procedures. Although this is certainly one of the central roles for teachers, recent trends in learning theory and practice suggest that facilitating learning may be more critical. That is, the way in which teachers perform their teaching role has a significant impact not only on how well students learn, but also on how motivated they are to learn.

OUR CHANGING NOTIONS OF TEACHERS' ROLES

Part of this changing notion of teachers' roles stems from an increased understanding of the learning process. Older, more traditional conceptions of learning placed primary responsibility for whether learning occurred on the teacher. Learning was viewed as a passive process that depended on teachers to present, structure, and convey information to students while students acted as "sponges" that absorbed the information pretty much as presented. Current conceptions of education now place the primary responsibility for learning on the student. Learning is viewed as an active, goal-directed process in which students transform and modify the information presented. They then construct new knowledge in ways that are uniquely meaningful to them.

According to current views of learning, students should have the responsibility for remembering and using information in ways that create permanent changes in their knowledge and skills. Students are expected to be self-directed, self-regulated, and self-motivated learners. Because students differ in their willingness and ability to assume this responsibility, you have the important role of helping to elicit and enhance students' natural motivation to learn and natural capacity to be self-determined.

There are two important ways in which you can do this. First, you can focus on helping students understand how their own thought processes work. This involves helping them understand the ways they may distort meanings based on their frame of reference and negative feelings, that is, the way their thought processes function at different mood levels. Second, you can provide an environment of adult caring and interest in which you validate your students' worth and significance and provide opportunities for relationship building. You need to create opportunities for youth to identify role models and experience mentoring relationships in a nurturing atmosphere of mutual caring and support.

The recommended approach here is to build on the assumption that bad moods, or insecure states of mind, are triggered when youth feel their survival or self-esteem is at stake. Once triggered, negative moods become self-confirming, biased information processing occurs, and these youth feel increasingly threatened and insecure. The intervention strategy is one that frees them to function in their natural state of mental health and motivation to learn rather than "fixing" them.

WHAT IT MEANS TO MOTIVATE STUDENTS

Think about what we have covered regarding the nature of motivation. What can interfere with or cover up the natural motivation to learn? What is the critical role you can play through the quality of your interactions with students? Some basic principles that emerge from research are:

1. Students are motivated by learning situations and activities that (a) challenge them to become personally and actively involved in their own learning and (b) allow them personal choice and control matched to their capabilities and to the task requirements.

2. Students' motivation is enhanced if they perceive that learning tasks (a) directly or indirectly relate to personal needs, interests, and goals and (b) are of appropriate difficulty levels so that they can accomplish them successfully.

3. Students' natural motivation to learn can be elicited in safe, trusting, and supportive environments characterized by (a) quality relationships with caring adults that see their unique potential, (b) learning and instructional supports that are tailored to students' unique learning needs, and (c) opportunities for students to take risks without fear of failure.

Thus, teaching must be a process that entices students to take control of their own learning, but that also provides levels of control that are appropriate to each student's ability to accomplish specific learning tasks.

These basic principles have a number of implications for the teacher's role as motivator. First, they imply that teachers need to get to know each student and their personal needs and interests. With this knowledge, the teacher is then in a position to provide individualized guidance about how students' personal goals fit in with learning goals established for the class. The teacher can also use this information about student needs and interests to structure educational goals and activities in such a way that each student can meet his or her own goals and experience success.

A second aspect of the teacher's role as implied by these principles is to focus on ways of challenging students both to take personal responsibility for their own learning and to be actively involved in their learning experiences. Knowing that students are naturally motivated to put time, effort, and energy into those areas that interest them or that are personally meaningful makes the job of challenging them that much easier. In addition, because students have a basic need to have some choice and control over learning activities in order to be maximally motivated, one set of effective strategies for challenging students involves providing them with opportunities to exercise personal control and choice over carefully selected task variables. Such variables could include the type of activity, level of mastery, amount of effort, or type of reward.

Finally, the principles imply that a big part of the teacher's role is to create a safe, trusting, and supportive climate by demonstrating genuine interest, caring, and concern for each student. The research suggests that part of what it takes to create a safe and secure climate for students is an emphasis on noncompetitive structures and learning goals as opposed to competitive structures and performance goals in which some students have to lose in order for some to win in the learning game. In order to ensure a safe and supportive climate it is also important to highlight the value of students' accomplishments, along with their unique skills and abilities, and the value of the learning process and learning tasks. Rewarding students' accomplishments, and encouraging them to reward themselves and take pride in their accomplishments, also creates a climate in which students feel cared about.

Your role as motivator, enhancing the development of students' positive sense of self and motivation for learning is an important, creative, and challenging one. Because learning is an active, goal-directed activity, you need to understand and capitalize on strategies for encouraging active, goal-directed thoughts and behaviors in students. You also need to help students understand their ability to create positive attitudes and change negative attitudes and beliefs about themselves and about learning.

SUMMARY

Goal 2 has focused on what the teacher's role as motivator means when seen from the perspective that students are naturally motivated to learn when they understand how negative thinking relates to low motivation to learn, pursue personally meaningful learning goals, and are supported by teachers in caring and respectful relationships. The specific motivational functions that follow from basic motivational principles and their implication for the role of teachers fall into five categories. These are the categories you will see spelled out in Goals 3 and 4, along with strategies and classroom activities that you can use to support your role as motivator. These functions are shown on the following page.

1. teaching students about how their thinking relates to moods and motivation, and about the control they have over such thoughts;

2. helping students value themselves, the learning process, and specific learning activities;

3. creating opportunities for students to pursue personally meaningful learning goals, thereby eliciting their natural tendencies to learn, grow, and take responsibility for their own learning;

4. encouraging academic risk taking to offset potentially negative consequences of the schooling experience such as boredom, fear of failure, and withdrawal; and

5. creating a positive climate of social and emotional support in which all students are individually and genuinely valued and respected.

At the end of Goal 2 is a list of suggested readings that provide you with other practical tips for succeeding in the role of motivator.

1 What do you consider the two most important ways in which teachers can act as motivators?

2 What do you think are the most important elements of a teacher's role in motivating students?

3 Have the aspects of the teacher's role as described here altered your view of what is essential to create a supportive and successful classroom environment? If so, how?

4 How has your interpretation of these concepts changed your response to the examples of Sasha and Derrin?

5 Describe ways in which the elements presented here could be used in your own classroom when teaching at-risk students.

ANSWERS TO QUESTIONS

1 Two key concepts you might have identified are the following:

a. Focus on helping youth understand how their own thought processes work.

b. Provide an environment of adult caring and interest.

2 Although answers will vary as to which of the 10 elements presented here are part of a teacher's role, many teachers will probably identify "diagnosing and understanding a student's unique needs, interests, and goals" as one of the most important.

3 Answers will vary.

4 Answers will vary; however, we hope they include trying to see things from Sasha's and Derrin's perspectives, building trust, and working with students to decide how to involve them in their own learning and how to meet their needs.

5 Answers will vary.

SUGGESTED READINGS

McCombs, B. L. (1988). Motivational skills training: Combining metacognitive, cognitive, and affective learning strategies. In C. E. Weinstein et al. (Eds.), *Learning and study strategies: Issues in assessment, instruction, and evaluation* (pp. 141–169). San Diego, CA: Academic Press.

McCombs, B. L., & Whisler, J. S. (1989). The role of affective variables in autonomous learning. *Educational Psychologist*, 24(3), 277–306.

Mills, R. C. (1990, June). *Substance abuse, dropout, and delinquency prevention: An innovative approach*. Paper presented at the 8th annual conference of the Psychology of Mind, St. Petersburg, Florida.

Mills, R. C., Dunham, R. G., & Alpert, G. P. (1988). Working with high-risk youth in prevention and early intervention programs: Toward a comprehensive model. *Adolescence*, 23(91), 643–660.

Peck, N., Law, A., & Mills, R. C. (1989). *Dropout prevention: What we have learned*. Ann Arbor, MI: ERIC Counseling and Personnel Services Clearinghouse.

Stewart, D. (1984, May). *The effect of teacher/student states of mind in raising reading achievement in high-risk, cross-cultural youth*. Paper presented at the 4th annual conference of Psychology of Mind, Honolulu, Hawaii.

Stewart, D. (1993). *Creating the teachable moment*. Blue Ridge Summit, PA: TAB Books.

Timm, J. (1992). *Self-esteem is for everyone (SEE) program*. Tampa, FL: Learning Advantages.

Timm, J., & Stewart, D. (1990). *The thinking teacher's guide to self-esteem*. Tampa: Florida Center for Human Development.

goal three

Helping Students
to Understand and Value Themselves

The next two sections, Goals 3 and 4, provide you with practical tools and tips for motivating hard to reach students. In Goal 3, we will focus on two important strategies that you can use with individual students to help enhance their self-motivation and overall self-development.

We will be looking at (a) helping students to understand their own psychological functioning and agency, that is, how their own thinking processes work, and (b) helping students value themselves and the learning process. These are key ele-

ments in reducing insecure thoughts and eliciting students'
natural motivation to learn and grow in positive ways. They
are also strategies you can use yourself to reduce stress and
burnout.

As discussed in previous sections, based on the ways
that quality relationships and relationships between
thinking and feeling can influence motivation to learn,
the best approaches for reaching hard to motivate students are those that "come from the heart." These are
approaches originated by teachers who are able to see
the potential mental health and natural motivation in
all students, who understand that negative feelings and
behaviors come from insecure thoughts, and who realize that they should not take these negative reactions
personally. From this perspective, teachers can genuinely respect and understand each student and trust their
own common sense to do what is most appropriate in
individual situations. At the same time, however, teachers need guidance in reaching this level of understanding, and it is to that end that the tips and tools in this
section are presented.

HELPING STUDENTS UNDERSTAND THEIR PSYCHOLOGICAL FUNCTIONING AND AGENCY

Teachers need to show students how their thinking
relates to their moods and motivation, and to demonstrate that students have control over thoughts that
affect their own motivation and learning. Because students are naturally motivated to learn when negative
thoughts and feelings about themselves and learning are
absent, teachers need to help students understand and
bypass or override these negative thoughts and feelings.
This involves providing students with direct instruction
in the basic principles of psychological functioning.

The following principles, taken from the work of Roger Mills, Darlene Stewart, and Jeffrey Timm (see the list of suggested readings at the end of Goal 1), can be taught to students:

> *Feelings originate in thoughts.* Feelings are an "inside job" and come from thoughts. If a student thinks, "School is boring and a waste of time," he or she will experience feelings ranging from apathy and boredom to anxiety and alienation. On the other hand, if a student thinks, "School is interesting and worth my time and effort," he or she will experience feelings ranging from excitement and interest to curiosity and attachment.

In other words, negative feelings come from negative thoughts and positive feelings come from positive thoughts.

> *You control your feelings.* If feelings come from thoughts and thoughts are generated by each person, each of us can control our feelings by controlling what we think. Feelings can't be forced on us from the outside; they come from inside. Sometimes it doesn't seem that way, particularly when our thoughts are heavily influenced by the values, opinions, or attitudes of other people or groups. For example, it's very common for young children to blame negative feelings on someone or something, as in, "She made me feel bad when she didn't invite me to her party." Now, it's true that someone may do something that prompts a negative thought on our part, but in this example, it's not what the person did that made this child feel bad. It was what he or she thought about what that person did. Not being invited to a party can generate thoughts like, "She invited everyone I know to her party. I feel really left out. She must not like me." It's that thought that produces the feelings of hurt, disappointment, and anger. On the other hand, if the child in our example had chosen to think, "It would be nice if I could be invited to that party, but it's not a big deal. I'm not going to let it get me down," his or her feelings would be a lot different.

What is important for you to remember as you teach your students about their thinking is that, as demonstrated above, negative thoughts produce negative feelings. Because each of us can control what we choose to think about a situation, we can also control our reactions to what we think; in other words, we can control our feelings. Even young children can be taught that negative feelings (e.g., being angry, sad, or fearful) tell us that we are thinking negative things (e.g., that someone deliberately tried to hurt us or that no one likes us). When we're feeling good, that usually means we are thinking positive thoughts.

The process of thinking creates our personal experience, our personal reality. Our thoughts are a very powerful tool. Even though we are often not aware of it, we are thinking all the time. When something happens, we make an instantaneous interpretation of what that event means. Regardless of whether or not that interpretation is true, we tend to believe what we think. For example, when a student won't stop talking in class, you automatically interpret what this behavior means. Your interpretation will be based on what you believe and have thought in the past. You might think, for example, "That student is being disrespectful." In turn, you feel angry or worried about how to react. The truth may be that there is a completely different reason, a reason that has nothing to do with you. By taking a moment to reflect and realize that the student may be following a natural impulse to be social or may be feeling insecure about him or herself, you can override your personal interpretation and correct the behavior without having negative feelings. Even students who are being disrespectful on purpose are reacting to negative thoughts and feelings. By learning not to take these reactions personally, you have a better chance of talking it out and not further alienating the student.

Students can learn to do the same thing. They can learn that their interpretations may have nothing to do with reality, then take time to consider other possibilities, and, as a result, learn not to take things personally.

A feeling of insecurity is the common denominator of low self-esteem and negative behavior. Most misbehavior in the classroom is the result of low self-esteem. Students, rather than being malicious, attention-seeking egomaniacs, are misbehaving because they're scared or insecure. Sometimes that's hard for adults to see, and it can be particularly difficult when working with elementary or middle school students. A friend snubs them, picks a fight, calls them names, and so on, and their typical reaction is to take it personally and react with negative feelings and actions. When we think about it, however, the negative behavior of both adults and youth can be traced to some kind of insecure feeling or insecure thought. The child who acts out in class may be insecure about his or her academic ability, social position, or any number of things that may be going on at school or at home.

Helping students understand that insecurity and low self-esteem underlie negative behavior can help them feel more empathy toward others. Knowing that they can learn to control their thoughts and feelings can also help them see that they can get back in touch with their natural self-esteem and motivation.

ACTIVITIES TO HELP STUDENTS UNDERSTAND THEIR PSYCHOLOGICAL FUNCTIONING AND AGENCY

Understanding the Thought Cycle

If students are to make use of the principles we have just discussed, they first need to understand how the thought cycle works. Figure 1 shows the ways that a student's thoughts affect his or her feelings and behavior, and the result in the classroom.

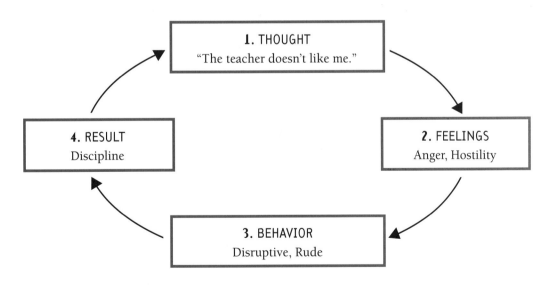

FIGURE 1 *The Thought Cycle*

In the example above, what started out as the student's thought that the teacher disliked him or her produced negative feelings of anger and hostility. In turn, these feelings produced disruptive and rude behavior in the classroom. The result was that the teacher disciplined the student. This all reinforced the student's thought that the teacher disliked him or her. The student proved his or her assumptions without ever realizing that the bad feelings started with his or her own thoughts!

A good activity for students is to discuss how this cycle works, generate examples of other thoughts (positive or negative), describe the feelings and behaviors these thoughts produce, and list what the results are likely to be. Once students see how this cycle works with different kinds of thoughts, they can do some individual or small group exercises to identify negative thoughts they have in certain situations (e.g., in relation to school, home, friends, etc.) and complete a Thought Cycle for each one. A copy that you can reproduce to use for exercises such as this is provided on the next page.

Before you use this exercise with students, it is important to see how it works for you. Think of a situation that "gets" you and work through a copy of the Thought Cycle. Think of some examples that you would be willing to share with your students.

THE THOUGHT CYCLE

Describe a situation that you don't like or that is a conflict for you at school, at home, with friends, etc. Then use the Thought Cycle diagram in Figure 2 to write out your thoughts, feelings, behavior, and the result in that situation. An example of a situation might be "having to get up early on Saturday mornings to help with household chores."

Situation: _____

_____

_____

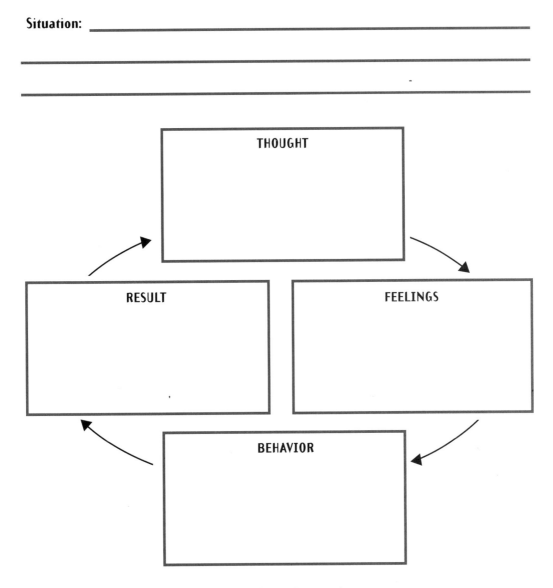

FIGURE 2 *The Thought Cycle: Completion Exercise*

Understanding the Principle of Separate Realities

Once students understand how the thought cycle works, they are ready to understand that each of us controls our feelings by controlling our thoughts. They can begin to see that everything starts with thought and that different people can have very different thoughts in the same situation. There are ways in which you can help students understand more fully the principle of separate realities. It is helpful to engage students in group discussions and have them generate their own examples of situations in which two people see things very differently. You can start with an example similar to the following.

EXAMPLE Tara and her mom have been fighting about whether she's old enough to wear make-up to school. Tara is 11 and most of her friends are allowed to wear eye make-up. Her mom thinks she should wait until she's 13 and in the 8th grade. Tara thinks that 11 is old enough because that's what others are doing. Tara and her mother have a conflict because they see things differently. They have different thoughts about the same situation.

Tara's mom has thoughts such as, "Wearing make-up before the eighth grade is just an invitation to boys that you want to be noticed and that's the start of trouble." When her mom thinks this, she feels upset, scared, and worried about her daughter. These feelings lead to her setting strict rules, yelling at Tara when she tries to argue with her, and grounding Tara when she talks disrespectfully to her.

Tara's thoughts are, "All my girlfriends' parents let them wear make-up to school. My mom is being unfair and old-fashioned. She doesn't understand me." When Tara thinks this way, she feels angry, resentful, and unhappy. These feelings lead to her arguing and yelling at her mom, crying, and talking disrespectfully. The result is that a big conflict exists, and the vicious cycle continues every time the topic of make-up comes up.

Helping students see how the principle of separate realities works is important in helping them see what causes conflicts between people and even between cultures. Classroom activities might include discussions such as the following:

Elementary

◻ What are the separate realities that cause brothers and sisters to disagree? (e.g., different views on sharing toys)

◻ What are the separate realities that cause conflicts between friends? (e.g., different views on what to do for fun)

◻ What are the separate realities that cause conflicts between neighbors? (e.g., different views on how often to mow the lawn or paint one's house)

◻ What are the separate realities that cause conflicts between people? (e.g., different views on how to drive)

Middle School and High School

◻ What are the separate realities that can cause men and women to disagree? (e.g., different views on kinds of jobs, roles in marriage, or time spent with other friends)

◻ What are the separate realities that cause conflicts between nations? (e.g., different views on territorial boundaries)

◻ What are the separate realities that cause conflicts between political parties? (e.g., different views on level of government control, help for poor people, or taxes)

◻ What are the separate realities that can cause conflicts between racial or ethnic groups? (e.g., different views on values that have an impact on how well they perform in different areas)

The Thought Cycle in Interpersonal Conflicts

Once students see how important an understanding of separate realities can be in their lives, they will be interested in knowing the ways the principle can help them with interpersonal conflicts that are caused by separate realities. An exercise that can be used is to have students work individually or in groups on "The Thought Cycle in Interpersonal Conflicts."

Let's start by looking at the following examples of negative thought cycles and how they can be broken. First, we'll discuss 9–year-old Lana and her mother. They are having a conflict about whether Lana is old enough to stay home alone the two nights per week that her mom gets home later than usual. Then we'll discuss 14–year-old Billy and his father. They are having a conflict about whether Billy is ready to learn to drive.

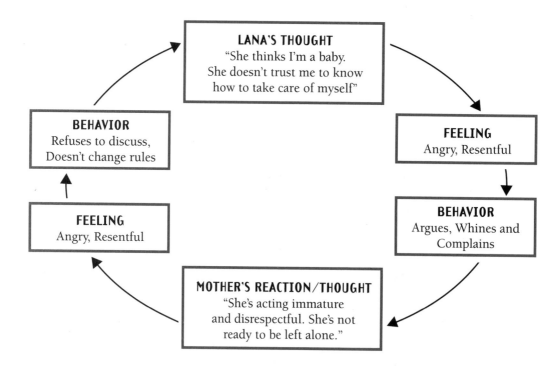

FIGURE 3 *Lana's Thought Cycle During a Conflict With Her Mother*

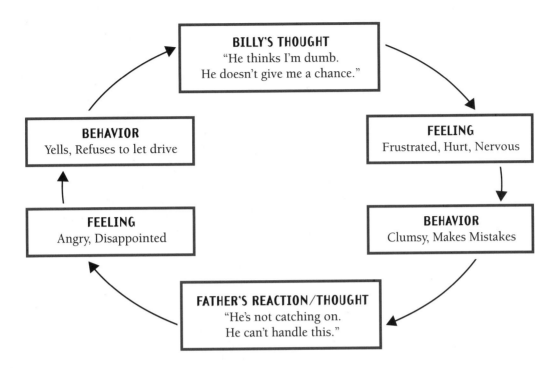

FIGURE 4 *Billy's Thought Cycle During a Conflict With His Father*

In these examples, Lana and Billy are feeling insecure, and their thoughts reflect this insecurity. But what also happens is that these insecure thoughts and feelings result in behaviors that support the thoughts. When Lana's mother and Billy's father see this behavior, each thinks their child may not be ready to engage in activities that require more maturity than Lana and Billy seem to demonstrate. Each parent's reaction reflects what he or she thinks and feels. In turn, this reinforces Lana's and Billy's thoughts. The vicious cycle goes on and on.

What students can be helped to see is that they can break the cycle by choosing to think differently about the situation. Figures 5 and 6 show how that can work in our examples of Lana and her mother and Billy and his father.

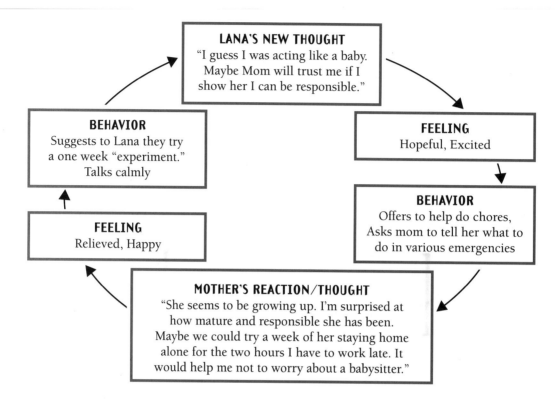

FIGURE 5 *Lana Breaks the Thought Cycle*

EXAMPLE Lana begins to understand that she'll get nowhere if she keeps getting angry at her mom and arguing, whining, and complaining. Lana decides that maybe she has been acting like a baby and that if she can show her mom that she can be responsible, her mom might change her mind about letting her stay home alone two nights per week when she's working late. Now Lana feels better and is even excited about showing her mom how grown up she can be. She starts doing more things around the house and takes responsibility for making sure she knows all the phone numbers and other things she should know in an emergency. Her mom sees these changes and decides to give Lana a chance to stay alone for two nights one week. Because her mom is feeling better, she is calmer and able to tell Lana about the experiment. Lana learned that she could choose to think about the situation differently and have better results.

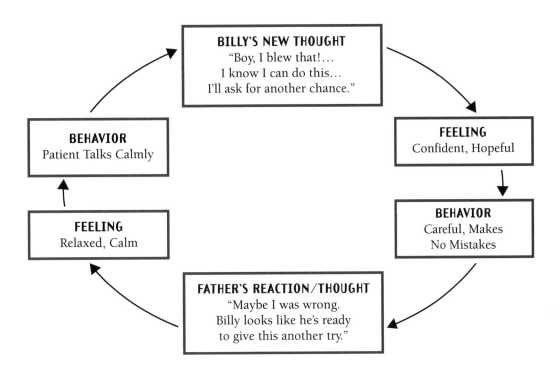

FIGURE 6 *Billy Breaks the Thought Cycle*

EXAMPLE Billy sees that his father is frustrated by how clumsy and uncoordinated he has been. He has the ability to choose to see how his thoughts contributed to the problem. He may think, "Boy, I blew that. This is silly. I know I can do this. I just need to explain to Dad that I was nervous, so I was letting what I thought he thought about me get in the way. I'll let him know I understand, and ask for another chance." Billy's feelings are now going to be different. Now he feels confident and hopeful. His behavior reflects these new feelings. As a result, his father thinks, "Maybe I was wrong. Billy looks like he's ready to give this another try." Then, his father will feel more relaxed and calm. As a result, Billy's father will probably be more patient and talk more calmly. That will further influence Billy's confidence, and a positive spiral will begin in the relationship! So, the problem started with only a thought, and the solution came when Billy took responsibility for choosing to view the situation differently and to change his thoughts about his father.

Students can be helped to work through personal examples or general examples from actual situations going on in the school or in the community. The "Thought Cycle in Interpersonal Conflicts" exercise in Figure 7 can be reproduced for student use. If the exercise is being used with students in the lower elementary grades, you may want to simplify the instructions.

The important part of the following exercise is that students understand that if they put themselves in the shoes of the person that they have a conflict with they are very likely to change their minds about the situation and the person. These different thoughts are the starting point for filling out this sheet a second time. Students should be reminded that although they cannot control what the other person thinks, feels, or does, choosing to think about the situation in a new way with new insights about the other person can change how we feel for the better.

As with the other exercises that we suggest for students, it is important for you to do these yourself first. Pick a conflict situation of your own and work through the "Thought Cycle in Interpersonal Conflicts" in two steps as described. Then you'll know firsthand how it can work.

THE THOUGHT CYCLE IN INTERPERSONAL CONFLICTS

Describe a conflict situation between you and another person. This person could be a friend, classmate, family member, teacher, or someone in your community. After describing the situation, write out your thoughts, feelings, and behavior, and how you think the other person reacted in terms of his or her thoughts, feelings, and behavior. Really try to put yourself in the other person's shoes. When you finish this sheet, ask yourself if you see the person or situation differently. Then fill out another "Thought Cycle in Interpersonal Conflicts" sheet, this time choosing to start with other thoughts that take into account your new thoughts about the person.

Situation: _____

_____

_____

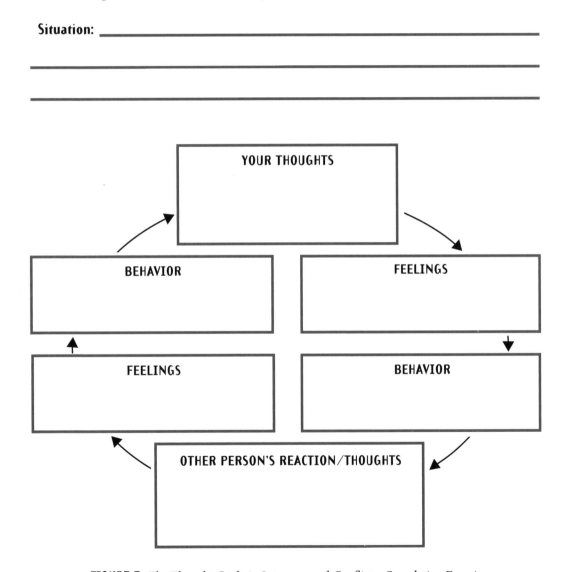

FIGURE 7 *The Thought Cycle in Interpersonal Conflicts: Completion Exercise*

Understanding Insecurity

By now, your students should be beginning to understand their basic psychological functioning and to see that they have control over creating their own thoughts and feelings. They are most likely beginning to understand that negative feelings about themselves also start with thoughts and that negative or insecure thoughts obscure their natural self-esteem. When students feel insecure, it can show up in many ways. Sometimes it shows up in aggressive behaviors, and other times it shows up in more passive or withdrawn behaviors.

The "Insecurity Checklist" on the following page is an exercise that can be helpful in recognizing when students are feeling insecure or when you, yourself, may be having insecure feelings. This exercise is taken from the "Self-Esteem Is for Everyone" program by Jeffrey P. Timm at the Florida Center for Human Development (see Suggested Readings at the end of Goal 2).

There are, obviously, many ways that activities such as the ones suggested here can be implemented with students of different ages and needs. You are the expert in choosing the ways in which the principles and examples provided here can best be applied. To give yourself a few ideas for using the tools you've seen so far, try the following exercises.

THE INSECURITY CHECKLIST

Everyone has feelings of insecurity at some time or another. Take a look at the checklist below and see if you can identify yourself in any of these. Check off the ones that you think apply (or have applied) to you. You don't have to feel insecure about doing this! You do not have to share it or show it to any one if you do not want to.

- ☐ Tongue-tied
- ☐ Shy
- ☐ Nerd
- ☐ Loudmouth
- ☐ Bully
- ☐ Know-it-all
- ☐ Goody-goody
- ☐ Complainer
- ☐ Heckler
- ☐ "I'm too good for this"
- ☐ Blamer
- ☐ Whiner
- ☐ Air head
- ☐ Wimp
- ☐ "I'm here but I'm not going to do anything"
- ☐ "I'll do anything if you will only like me"
- ☐ "I have to get an 'A' or my life is over"

The Insecurity Checklist is the copyrighted material of Learning Advantages.
It has been used with the written consent of Jeffrey P. Timm, the author.

1   Generate an example of how you could show your students the "Thought Cycle." Include some examples of situations that they don't like or that demonstrate conflicts.

2   Plan a class discussion for your students that would help them understand the principle of separate realities.

HELPING STUDENTS VALUE THEMSELVES AND LEARNING

The second important strategy that teachers can use to help individual students enhance their self-motivation and overall self-development is to teach them to value themselves, the learning process, and specific learning activities. Students' understanding of their own thought processes can help them see their inherent worth and natural motivation to learn. Beyond this important first step, it is important that teachers personally get to know each student while also helping all students define their interests and goals.

Below we have listed some specific ways of doing this. These strategies can help you to learn more about each student and to make learning activities more relevant and meaningful for each student. Examples of activities follow a discussion of the strategies.

Strategies for Meeting Individual Learning Needs

Diagnosing Students' Unique Needs, Interests, and Goals

Surveys or personal interviews are good ways to find out about the unique needs, interests, and goals of each student. Information from surveys and interviews can be supplemented by background or demographic information from student files, as well as observations of student behavior and performance.

Some examples of student interest surveys are included in this section. You may use these or modify them to fit the particular needs of your students.

Helping Students to Define Their Personal Goals and Relate Them to Learning Goals

Goal setting, a process similar to problem solving, is easily taught and learned. This process can be taught to students individually or as a group or class activity. Goal setting not only helps students better define what is important to them, but it also helps them learn to value activities that help them reach their goals. In addition, students gain related skills in decision making, risk and benefit evaluation, and progress evaluation while they are learning the goal setting process.

Relating General Learning Goals to Students' Unique Interests and Goals

It is in this area that your creativity as a teacher has a chance to shine! Once you know your students, individually and as a group, you and only you are in the best position to see how the general learning goals for your grade level or content area could be related to student goals and interests. An idea that usually works well is to get the students themselves involved in finding ways to make content more relevant to their interests and goals. Student-generated projects within a general topic area can help students not only to match their interests with learning goals, but also to achieve greater personal responsibility for their own learning. To accomplish this, students may need explicit training in how to relate their interests and goals to learning content and learning activities.

Structuring Learning Goals and Activities to Foster Individual Student Success

An important finding that has emerged from the work of Carol Dweck and her colleagues is that adaptive belief patterns that contribute to a higher motivation to learn include establishing learning goals rather than performance goals. What this means is that if students can be encouraged to set goals for what they personally want to learn or accomplish, they will be more motivated and will achieve more than if they set goals for simply being able to perform better than others in their class. When students are encouraged to compete against themselves, not others, and to strive for learning rather than performance goals, motivation and achievement are enhanced. Strategies such as cooperative learning, in which students work together to accomplish similar learning goals, are good examples of ways to help students focus on their own learning.

Another important step in helping students meet their own goals and experience success is the individualization of learning goals and activities so that they are matched to unique student capabilities as well as interests and goals. This matching process ideally results in each student being able to demonstrate competence and experience learning success.

Using Modeling to Instruct Students in the Value and Benefits of Specific Accomplishments

One of life's best teachers is a model. We often learn by watching others. When you, as a teacher, model excitement and enthusiasm about various subject areas, the value of those areas is apparent. Similarly, when you model expertise in various areas, you are demonstrating the value of accomplishments. You can also model and instruct students in the value and benefits of the learning process itself, as it relates to the accomplishment of personal goals and the value of the specific learning task in accomplishing these goals. We've all had the experience of being taught by someone who loved his or her subject and students. This was the teacher from whom we learned the most. It may have even been that teacher who helped us to love math when we thought we hated it and couldn't do it.

A big part of your role will be modeling the process of monitoring your thoughts and moods, defining and setting learning goals, structuring activities for reaching these goals, and becoming an expert in the goal area selected. Now let's take a look at some specific activities and tools you can use to help students value themselves and learning.

ACTIVITIES TO HELP STUDENTS VALUE THEMSELVES AND THE LEARNING PROCESS

Identifying Student Interests and Goals

In order to help students value themselves, you first need to diagnose individual students' needs, interests, and goals. You also need to help students self-assess their interests and goals so that they may develop higher level metacognitive processes of self-awareness, self-understanding, self-monitoring, and self-management.

Student interest surveys are a valuable tool for helping you learn more about individual students' interests as well as assist them in their own self-assessment. These are effectively used in individual or group settings, particularly if students trust you and understand the rationale for providing information about their interests. Following up with individual talks or informal interviews is another good way to establish rapport if students sense your genuine interest, respect, and caring.

EXAMPLE Ms. Parker was a fourth grade teacher in a suburban middle school. It was near the end of August, and she was getting ready for the new school year and 28 new students.

"I wonder what neat interests and talents this class will have?" she thought to herself. "I need to figure out some fun ways to get to know this special bunch."

She had found a good interest survey but she wanted to be sure the kids didn't feel threatened about completing it. She began planning some fun "ice breaker" introductions for the first day of class in which students would introduce themselves and share something about themselves that they wanted everyone to know. This would be followed up by a memory game, some prizes, and some treats. When everyone was feeling good, Ms. Parker would suggest that she'd love to know more about each of her students so that she could make sure this school year would be fun and interesting for them. She would ask the class if that was okay with them, and, assuming it was, she would hand out the survey for them to complete. She would be sure to let them know that they only needed to share things they felt comfortable sharing. She then made plans for how she would follow up the survey activities with some special private talk time with each student.

This is one example of how a teacher could use an interest survey. There are many adaptations that you could make to meet the needs of your students, and there are no doubt some refinements you will want to make to the sample surveys on the following pages.[3] The important thing is for you to come up with activities you feel comfortable doing to get to know your students. For this reason, it is a good idea for you to "play student" and take the surveys yourself. That's a good way to make sure the items will be at the right level and in the right language for your students.

[3] The example surveys on the following pages are reprinted with permission from Whisler, J. S., & McCombs, B. L. (1992). *A middle school self-development advisement program*. Aurora, CO: Midcontinent Regional Educational Laboratory.

STUDENT INTEREST SURVEY—What I Do for Fun

Name:

UNFINISHED SENTENCES: Complete each of the unfinished sentences below with the first thought that comes to your mind. Your answers can be either a positive or negative statement.

1 | My hobbies are

2 | The types of things I like to do with other people are

3 | The things I do for fun are

4 | The things I do to relax are

5 | When I need to get away from it all I

6   I feel good when

7   The type of present I would most like to receive would be

8   If I had an extra $10, I would

9   If I had an extra $50, I would

10   If I had an extra $100, I would

11   I spend money every week on

12   Of the things I do every day, I would hate to give up

STUDENT INTEREST SURVEY—Completely Me

Name:

Incomplete sentences allow you to get more insight into yourself when you complete them with whatever pops into your head first. Complete the sentences below with the first thing that comes to your mind.

1 I am happiest when I

2 The best thing about me is

3 The worst thing about me is

4 My favorite _____ is

5 If I could have one wish it would be

6 I get angry when

7 A thought I keep having is

8 Something I've never told anyone about before is

9 I feel important when

10 I don't like to

11 I seem to get my way when

12 The thing I'm most concerned with is

13 I am

14 If I were the president, the first thing I would do is

15 One question I have about life is

STUDENT INTEREST SURVEY—Skills and Abilities I'd Love to Have

Name:

Imagine that someone has invented a way to enable you to develop new skills or abilities—or improve ones you already have—to the point that you would be an expert. Take a minute and fantasize what it might be like if you could be the very best at anything and everything. List 10 skills and abilities you would develop or improve if there were no limits.

1 _____

2 _____

3 _____

4 _____

5 _____

6 _____

7 _____

8 _____

9 _____

10 _____

Now think of someone you admire—living or not, famous or not—who is really good at one of the skills or abilities you listed. Write that person's name and his/her skill below. Then write what it is about the person you admire.

1 The person is

2 His/her ability/skill is

3 What I admire about this person is

STUDENT INTEREST SURVEY—The Story of My Life

Name:

Things we think about and goals we make for ourselves often come true. That's because we dream about them and imagine them really happening. Write a "dream" story that you'd like to have come true in your life.

1 In the year   , I was born in   (city).

2 Even as a child, I really liked to

and

3 I wanted to become the best

4 As a teenager, I like to

and

5 In school my favorite subjects were

and

6 When others tried to get me to do things I didn't want to do I

7 I saw myself as

8 Others saw me as a person who

9 When I got close to graduating from high school, I decided to

because

10 When I was 20, I

11 When I was 30, I

12 In fact, I became the kind of person

13 The most important things I accomplished were

14 The most important people in my life were

15 The ways I am different from the way I am now are

Helping Students to Set Goals

Once both you and your students have a clearer idea of their interests and goals, it's a good time to talk about how they can achieve those goals. Achieving personal goals is not something only a few people can do. It's possible for everyone. Goal setting is basically a simple planning process that can be learned. Students need to understand that goal setting is important because it will give them a strategy for making their dreams come true, for going after the things they want. By setting and achieving goals, people can avoid lives without a purpose or direction. They can make the most of their lives.

What is also important for students to understand is that goal setting sets up positive expectations and demonstrates that individuals are in control of their own lives. It helps students take responsibility for controlling the direction in which they want to go and what they want to accomplish. When students learn to set goals and to plan the accomplishment of these goals, they realize that they have the power to decide what to do or what to accomplish. They don't have to let other people or things decide for them. Allowing students opportunities to set goals and plan activities, events, or other aspects of their school life is a way to help them learn responsibility, understand their personal agency, and become more self-directed and healthy human beings.

A simple **goal-setting process** has the following steps:

☐ Define your goal clearly

☐ List steps to take to reach this goal

☐ Think of problems that might come up that would interfere

☐ Think of solutions to these problems

◻ Set a timeline for reaching the goal

◻ Evaluate your progress

◻ Reward yourself for accomplishments

In the beginning, teaching this process can be accomplished as a class activity. Once students understand how to use the process, they can apply it to their personal goals. To help students apply the process, have them pick the domain (e.g., home, school, friends, and hobbies) and then teach them the following simple mnemonic device:

A goal should be

Achievable (reasonable for your age and strengths)
Believable (you need to believe you can accomplish it)
Conceivable (clearly stated and measurable)
Desirable (you really want it, and others want it for you)

Students can use the "**A**, **B**, **C**, **D**" mnemonic device to evaluate their personal goals. They can then go on to use the process for academic goals.

1. Develop a plan for how you would get to know the students in your classroom.

2. Pick one of the sample interest surveys and describe how you would modify it for your students.

3. Design a classroom activity for teaching goal setting to your students.

Relating Interests and Goals to Learning

Having helped students identify their individual interests and goals, you are now in a better position to promote the next important motivational strategy: helping students value the learning process and specific learning activities. In order to do this, you will need to know (a) strategies for relating general learning goals to students' unique interests and goals and (b) strategies for structuring learning goals and activities so that each student can accomplish his or her own goals and experience success.

A quality student–teacher relationship is one in which each person recognizes and acknowledges each other's area of expertise. The student is the one most knowledgeable about areas of interest and goals. The teacher is the one who has a clear idea of the educational content and is able to identify the key learning components or skills that should be a part of the educational plan. The teacher is also the one who has had past experience in helping students develop projects that incorporate specific interests and at the same time meet educational objectives. Figure 8 provides a graphic example of these areas of expertise.

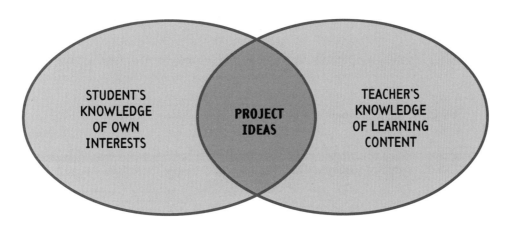

Recognizing the Overlap of Student and Teacher Expertise

FIGURE 8 *The Relationship Between the Student's Areas of Interest and Goals and the Teacher's Knowledge of Learning Content*

In an interest survey, a seventh-grade student has identified several areas of interest: music, girls, and skateboarding. The current mathematics class unit is fractions. The key educational components in the fractions unit are scale and ratio. The end objectives of the unit are to enable students to use fractions and their understanding of ratio to solve problems in model size and actual object size using basic fraction skills (i.e., adding, subtracting, multiplying, and dividing). The challenge for you as a teacher is to find ways to relate this student's interests to what needs to be learned. If you know the interests of all the students in a class you can find ways of placing students with similar interests into the same problem solving groups.

A matrix can be used to identify ways in which student interests and goals can be correlated with educational objectives. This is the first step in identifying an educational plan for the student that is self-motivating and at the same time meets the educational objectives of the teacher. Although it may seem that this approach to lesson design could add time to the project that would be better spent on actual project construction, in reality, the easiest point at which to make major project decisions is in the planning stage. With the matrix design method, it is relatively simple to see if there are indeed areas of correlation between interests and learning goals. If the matrix shows no correlation, the student interest survey can be refined, rewritten in a more comprehensive manner, or readministered to students with some direction by the teacher. In this example, the matrix might appear as shown in Figure 9.

When viewed this way, many correlations become obvious. However, let's set some learning and performance goals that combine skateboarding interest with the problem solving skill of model size and the basic fraction skill of multiplying fractions.

Through negotiation, the student and teacher may decide that the individual plan will be to design and construct one-quarter scale models of skateboards. Once the project has been defined, its implementation

PROJECT DESIGN MATRIX						
Educational Objectives-Ratio and Scale						
	PROBLEM SOLVING		BASIC FRACTION SKILLS			
	Model Size	Actual Size	Add	Subtract	Multiply	Divide
Music						
Girls						
Skateboarding	X				X	

FIGURE 9 *Project Design Matrix for Correlating Student's Interests With Educational Objectives*

could take several forms. If the teacher recognizes that it is the final result or final project that is the real measure of whether or not the student has acquired the basic skills, he or she may elect to allow the student to go ahead and develop construction drawings. If it is apparent from the student's drawings that he or she already has the necessary understanding of problem solving using multiplication of fractions, then the student could be allowed to pursue actual construction. If the student experiences problems in developing the drawing set, then the teacher can intervene and provide the needed instruction to give the student the appropriate skills.

This does not imply that the teacher must find time to spend with each and every student teaching basic skills. Through careful scheduling, all students would be taking part in the interest survey–educational content–matrix development process at the same time. Project ideas could be a group brainstorming process, each student offering and receiving suggestions on possibilities. The period of class time that is actually devoted to the study of the required basic fraction skills would be common for all students, but would be attended only by those actually needing the additional instruction.

Although the benefits of this process are many, one of the most important is that the student has a higher level of value for the learning process and the specific learning activity. Why? Because the project is now personally relevant to the student, and the teacher has shown that he or she respects and values the student's individual needs and interests.

1 Using the student interest in skateboards, identify a correlation with different educational objectives listed, and then propose a student project that might be appropriate.

2 Using the matrix in the example, identify a correlation other than that with skateboarding. Propose a student project.

3 Using the matrix approach, think of one of your students for whom you can identify some areas of interest. Relate these interests to a set of educational objectives in your field, and describe how you would develop an appropriate project for that student.

Modeling the Value of Learning

Finally, as we mentioned in the previous section, the best teacher is a good model. Students learn by watching others and particularly from watching their teachers! Some of the many ways you can be a good model are by demonstrating

☐ excitement about the subject matter,

☐ expertise in different areas,

☐ the value of accomplishments,

☐ personal responsibility for learning,

☐ the benefits of the learning process,

☐ respect and genuine regard for others, and

☐ the importance of risk taking.

Let's take a look at a couple of examples of how these values and qualities can be modeled by teachers in the classroom.

EXAMPLE Mr. Oslo loves science, and he loves kids. His goal is to inspire students' interest in finding answers to questions by using scientific methods. In his second-grade class, most of his students are curious about something and are always asking questions. Whenever they ask a question, he "becomes a scientist." Like a character in a play, he acts out the part. He puts on his special white coat, adopts a serious but enthusiastic pose, and moves through the process of using scientific methods in "discovering" the answer to the student's question. Sometimes he gets the student who asked the question, the whole class, or small groups of students involved in becoming scientists and finding their own answers to the question. His classes are fun, interesting, and inspiring. All his students talk about what a good teacher Mr. Oslo is. Many of them have gone on to careers in science.

EXAMPLE | Ms. Vernon is an eighth-grade teacher who really loves learning. She reads all the time in all kinds of areas such as history, literature, psychology, and world affairs. She also reads fiction and nonfiction. Her love of learning has opened many doors in life for her. Even though she can't afford to travel around the world, she has traveled around the world in her mind through the adventures and information in books. Her eighth-grade social studies class is lucky. She has found all kinds of ways to make topics they are studying come alive by bringing in sections of books on many related issues. Her excitement about how these topics can be enriched by bringing in outside materials is catching. She encourages and challenges the students in her class to bring in things they have read that are of personal interest and related to the topic they are covering. She rewards their accomplishments in class as well as those outside readings they do that are relevant to the class. Her students leave her class knowing much more than social studies and valuing much more than what they learned in her class. They have found what it means to value the learning process.

SUMMARY

The strategies presented in Goal 3 have focused on things you can do to help students uncover their natural motivation and begin to grow and develop in positive ways in spite of negative life experiences and negative ways that they may have learned to view themselves and their abilities to learn. By helping students understand how their own thinking contributes to their feelings and motivation, and by providing opportunities for students to personalize learning, you can begin to see that natural motivation emerge. The activities and strategies suggested here are intended to help you think of new ways to deal with students who seem to have lost their motivation to learn. They involve helping students to understand themselves and their own thinking. They also involve helping students begin to revalue learning by seeing how it relates to their personal interests and goals.

1 List the areas that you would like to model.

2 Write out the ways you currently model these areas.

3 List any changes you plan to make in how you will model the areas you have chosen.

goal four

Creating a Classroom Environment
That Motivates Students

In this section we will focus on classroom strategies that establish a motivational climate for learning. There are three important ways in which this can be done, and we will examine each of these in the following pages. First, you can create opportunities for students to express self-determination by encouraging their natural tendencies to learn, grow, and take responsibility for their own learning. Second, you can encourage students to take academic risks. This helps offset potentially negative consequences of the schooling experience, such as boredom, fear of failure, and withdrawal. Last, but not least, you can create a positive climate of social support in which all students are individually and genuinely valued and respected.

CREATING OPPORTUNITIES FOR GROWTH AND SELF-DETERMINATION

The teacher as motivator creates opportunities that draw out students' natural tendencies to learn, grow, and take responsibility for their own learning. Though it may sound simple, this strategy is not always easy to accomplish. In essence, it involves structuring one's teaching approach to encourage student choice.

To create opportunities for self-determination, you have to take a risk; you have to be willing to reexamine older, traditional beliefs about teacher control versus student control. Allowing students some control does not translate into an "anything goes" classroom. It does mean that students experience personal control and you provide opportunities for them to be co-contributors in their own learning process. Once you understand how important it is for students to have personal control and self-determination and to take increased responsibility for their own learning, changing these beliefs becomes more palatable.

The Teacher as Facilitator Versus Knowledge Base

As traditional concepts of the student as passive receptor of knowledge have changed, views about teachers as the source of knowledge are also changing. Teachers are seeing themselves more as a resource for helping students access knowledge and as a guide for helping students learn to use appropriate information management tools. Your ability to facilitate self-directed learning by the student will be more important in the classroom. The concept of teachers and students empowering each other, being colearners and taking risks together, extends the bounds of the traditional classroom.

The Teacher as Instructional Designer

If self-direction through personal goal setting is to take place, you will be under increased pressure to identify topics that may be relevant to individual students, while also addressing agreed-on content and performance standards. The traditional use of a textbook to define the subject areas of a class may not provide the degree of diversity needed to find a topic of personal value. Once a topic is defined collaboratively by you and the student, consideration must be given to the plan of action the student will follow to complete his or her study and to convey the information to you and the class. A variety of instructional settings may need to be available to accommodate the unique characteristics of different study topics. Settings might include both independent and cooperative group work areas.

The Student as an Expert in His or Her Field

As students take more responsibility for the definition of personal educational goals and become more actively involved in personally relevant learning activities, and as their self-motivation takes over, they will be challenged to become experts in the field of study they have chosen. You will again be taking a risk in acknowledging that students may have become more knowledgeable than you are in selected topics. You will then have the opportunity to take on the role of the learner and model what it is like to share expertise in positive ways. You and your students will have an opportunity to develop skills in managing your relationship in a positive and constructive manner.

The Student as Conveyor of Knowledge

The entire class benefits from the self-directed study performed by individual students. Students, given proper skills, can share their newfound knowledge. They will, however, discover that it may not be as easy on the other side of your desk as they might have thought. To make the sharing experience positive, you will need to assist students in developing methods of sharing their knowledge, both inside and outside of the classroom, that make the experience a positive and empowering one. Because schools are increasingly emphasizing learning outcomes such as contributing to the community, you will have more opportunities to help students develop skills for presenting what they are learning to community members and parents.

Activities to Promote Students' Growth and Self-Determination

As we have discussed, teachers need to understand their roles as (a) facilitator versus knowledge base, (b) instructional designer, and (c) model in showing students how to become experts and to share their knowledge. The learning environment should place responsibility on the students for their own educational plans. Students will become self-directed and self-motivated only when they have personal control over their education. This implies that much of the information gathering will be the responsibility of the student.

Giving students responsibility for their own learning prevents two problems with the teacher-centered approach to conveying information. First, it prevents the low levels of learning that can occur when students assume little responsibility for developing the skills needed to search for and process relevant information. Second, and more important, it prevents delivery of the message implicitly given in a teacher-centered approach that the teacher has all of the knowledge about a topic. This is not the way things work in the real world. In truth, when the working person needs information, he or she will use a number of different sources to gather all of the information needed.

Giving students appropriate levels of responsibility for their own learning does not mean that there will not be times when the teacher needs to conduct a specific whole group lesson on a topic. In the example of correlating student interests in skateboarding with a math lesson on ratio and scale given earlier, the teacher needed to present a lesson on fractions and scale in order to ensure that the students had the basic skills they needed to develop a project.

What giving students more control and responsibility in the learning process does mean, however, is that you have a new responsibility to be aware of all of the ways to access sources of information. Many of these sources may not be within the school. Facilitating active student learning will also involve providing the methods with which to access and retrieve outside sources of information. Being a facilitator also means you can help the student develop the ability to be selective regarding what kinds of, how much, and in what ways information is retrieved when working on particular topics or projects. Once the walls of the school are eliminated as a barrier to knowledge, the problem may become one of having far too much information to process. As students acquire the skills they need to assume greater responsibility for their own learning, the classroom can become the place where the student also learns important information management skills. These skills can be taught as an educational topic appropriate for whole group instruction.

EXAMPLE In an interest survey, an eighth-grade student has identified several areas of interest: boys, a specific rock group, becoming a banker, and learning about her father's native country of Mexico. The current social studies class unit is the study of economics. A general introduction to economics has been given. The teacher would like to develop student projects that address one or more of the following subtopic areas: third world nations, education levels of the population, per capita income total, per capita income by career or trade, gross domestic product (GDP), birth and death rates, and life expectancy. After negotiation, the student has decided to complete a project that compares the banking system in Mexico with the systems in the United States and in South Africa. In doing this project, she will examine education levels, per capita income, and life expectancy in these countries to determine what similarities and differences exist. The teacher suggests several sources of information that can be used in this project, including local bankers in the community, and works with the student in developing a plan for getting the information she needs.

As a *facilitator*, then, the teacher now has the responsibility of directing the student to different sources of information. The student may elect to use traditional media-center-printed sources of data. She may instead elect to use a commercially available software database such as MECC DataQuest, or may choose to use the school telecommunications center to dial an on-line information source. In deciding what information can be obtained from local bankers, the student may want to construct an interview form. The student's source selection will have implications for what additional skills the teacher must instruct. In order to teach these kinds of skills to elementary school students, teachers will first need to provide opportunities for students to become aware of and understand different sources of information (e.g., libraries, computers) and how to access and use these sources. As schools move toward placing greater emphasis on information access skills, coordinated curricula are being developed that meet students' developmental needs in acquiring these skills.

As an *instructional designer*, the teacher must monitor progress, provide encouragement and guidance, and identify supplemental sources of information if necessary. Returning to our example of the eighth-grade student and her project on comparing banking systems, once the student has progressed beyond the information gathering stage, the teacher will need to assist the student in synthesizing the information. There are many ways to look at the data to see what similarities and differences exist. The student will most likely need assistance from the mathematics teacher to complete numerical analysis and then additional guidance from the social studies teacher to interpret the numerical results. Once the analysis is complete, some method must be developed to compile a complete project and present the findings to the class. This may lead to instruction in using the computer as a presentation device to graphically display correlations between economic factors, or the use of the visual arts teacher as a resource for developing pictorial representations of data correlations. All of these considerations indicate a further responsibility on the part of the social studies teacher to find a way to do interdisciplinary teaching with support from other members of the teaching staff. The student benefits by seeing real world relationships among academic areas.

In this example it is easy to see that the student, with proper facilitation, can become an expert in her particular field of interest. By having access to such a variety of data, and by concentrating on areas of specific personal interest, the student has been motivated to expand her knowledge beyond that of the teacher.

The opportunity is now presented for the student to share her knowledge and become the teacher. Because the teacher is no longer the "expert" on the specific topic, it is logical for the true expert to present the information to the class. In addition, through the teacher's sharing of expertise on teaching, the student can be taught the skills necessary to provide a complete social studies lesson about her particular area of interest in a way that is interesting and exciting to the rest of the class.

1 List possible sources of information about the banking systems in various countries, including economic factors being studied in the example given above.

---

2 Create a project design matrix using the student areas of interest and social studies topic areas listed above. Use the matrix to design a student project that does not use the father's native country as the student's area of interest. Use one or more of the economics topics.

---

3 Is it possible to design a project from the information in the example above that focuses on the student's interest in boys? If so, what would the project be? If not, how could you as the teacher propose to expand the economic objectives to include topics that could be used to develop a student project?

---

4 Identify a set of educational objectives that could be used for a unit in your class. Develop a list of likely student interests. Combine the two into a project design matrix. Briefly propose a student project. What sources of information would you suggest to the student? What skills would you as the teacher need to provide to allow the student to synthesize and analyze the information gathered? What suggestions would you make to the student in order to enable him or her to make an interesting presentation to the class?

ENCOURAGING ACADEMIC RISK TAKING

Our next motivational strategy goes hand-in-hand with students taking responsibility for their own learning and personal growth. You also need to encourage students to develop the personal and academic skills to become academic risk takers. This helps to offset the potentially negative consequences of the schooling experience such as boredom, fear of failure, and withdrawal.

In order to encourage risk taking, you need to genuinely respect and appreciate students' individual differences and unique accomplishments. You also need to know how to help students identify appropriate rewards and help them systematically and realistically reward themselves for their accomplishments.

Strategies for Encouraging Academic Risk Taking Through Modeling

You can demonstrate that the classroom is a safe environment in which to share new knowledge. It is most important that you avoid "put downs" and value each student's unique accomplishments. You can also set a tone that discourages negative comments from other students. When asked a question about which you are unsure, if you feel comfortable (a) admitting that you don't know the answer and (b) asking the students to give their opinions, you are modeling an effective way to deal with the situation. If you are comfortable with sharing this lack of knowledge with the class, everyone will gain by researching the real answers, and the process will model an effective way of dealing with the classroom when it becomes the students' turn to share what they have learned about their topic of interest. These modeling strategies for encouraging academic risk taking impact both students and teachers. Both will be teachers and learners, learning to take risks in the process.

Strategies for Encouraging Acceptance of Success

Students not only fear failure, but they are also often fearful of academic success due to peer pressure. For example, if the peer culture is one that marks the top achievers as "nerds," students who value peer acceptance over academic achievement will deliberately perform below their ability. Students need to develop skills in sharing their knowledge and presenting their findings to others in ways that value each student's unique talents and contributions. You, along with your students, need to develop techniques that allow sharing in a positive and constructive environment. For example, when students can demonstrate that their individual projects have been in response to their individual interests and that their interests may be similar to those of others, everyone can gain a feeling of educational growth in personally relevant areas.

Strategies for Assessing Unique Accomplishments

If you are no longer directing students toward a specific topic or specific approach to take in developing a project, traditional methods for evaluating student work may not be valid. In fact, the national trend toward alternative forms of assessment that measure individual student growth are a reflection of this type of change in assessment methods. Further, there is increasing recognition that student motivation will be maintained at high levels when the student knows that his or her end product will be assessed in a way that is appropriate. That means that you may need to develop a variety of assessment tools such as portfolios and performance-based measures that help students assess individual growth and achievement of learning goals.

Strategies for Helping Students Choose Appropriate Rewards

Grades may still motivate many students, but for those who do not see traditional grading scales as relevant, new systems of rewards must be developed. Students are the best source of information about the kinds of rewards that are personally meaningful. You take an additional risk in allowing students to choose their own rewards, but many teachers who have been willing to involve students in this process have been surprised at the results. When students have had positive learning experiences, feel valued and respected, and have some control over their own learning, the rewards they choose tend to be those that further their learning or that provide recognition for their accomplishments. For example, students may choose rewards such as opportunities to perform projects with people they admire in their communities, take special field trips, or demonstrate what they know and can contribute in parent–teacher meetings.

Activities to Encourage Academic Risk Taking

The activities we will describe in this section illustrate four important aspects of promoting academic risk taking: (a) encouraging academic risk taking through modeling, (b) developing students' abilities to accept success, (c) assessing or evaluating unique projects and accomplishments, and (d) developing students' abilities to select appropriate rewards or recognition.

Particularly for upper elementary, middle school, and high school students, participating in a more open, self-directed environment in a way that is positive and constructive will require some new learning and some practice. Self-regulation, or the directing of one's own learning, is a learned skill. An effective way for you to offer both instruction and practice would be to model introductory sections of the unit to be taught. The period of introduction may also be an opportunity for you to demonstrate that your knowledge is not total and, in fact, often leads to many interesting questions about the topic that might be of personal interest to students. The introductory section may actually generate a number of ideas for student projects.

EXAMPLE A science teacher is about to begin a unit on energy, energy history, traditional energy sources, alternative energy sources, energy uses, energy conservation, and the impact of energy generation on the environment. By this time the students have developed more refined skills in completing their interest surveys and are better able to describe their likes and dislikes. In addition, the teacher has encouraged the students to complete personal interest surveys that deal directly with the forms of written and spoken expression that the students have been studying in language arts and to select the one form that is the most interesting to each student. The science teacher and language arts teacher have coordinated their lessons and plan to focus on several specific expressive skills: formal oral report, oral demonstration, story telling, debate, drama, role playing, written short stories, business letters, research papers, poetry, and written essay. One student has indicated a particular interest in expression through poetry.

To model the process, the teacher has also completed a personal interest survey, has outlined the educational objectives of the energy history unit, and has constructed a project design matrix to share with the class, such as the one shown in Figure 10.

The teacher shows the students that by using the matrix, they can make a collaborative decision such as presenting a project on energy history that will use role playing as the presentation method. Let's see how the example plays out.

PROJECT DESIGN MATRIX	Energy History	Traditional Energy Sources	Alternative Energy Sources	Energy Uses	Energy Conservation	Energy and the Environment
Formal oral report						
Oral demonstration						
Story stelling						
Debate						
Drama						
Role playing						
Written short story						
Business letter						
Research paper						
Poetry						
Written essay						

FIGURE 10 *Using a Project Design Matrix to Encourage Student Choice: Students Select the Language Skills They Will Use to Present Material on Energy History*

EXAMPLE	THE SCIENCE CLASS

Day One

It was the first day of a new semester. Ms. Snyder, the science teacher, knowing that she would be able to get students' attention if she gave them a few minutes to chat with friends they haven't seen since school let out last June, simply waited two or three minutes. When the chatter slowed down, she asked, "Have you ever wondered what your great-grandparents did when they needed to see in order to do something after the sun had set?" There was a hush in the room as each student attempted to figure out where this conversation was headed.

Ms. Snyder went on to say, "We know that they did not have the advantage of walking over to the light switch on the wall and turning on the electric lamp. They must have had to do something different than what we are used to. Does anyone have an idea what they might have done to give them some light to read or work by?" At first, most of the students were reluctant to risk giving an answer that might appear to be foolish. By waiting and allowing the students a great deal of time to ponder the question and, coincidentally, by giving the students the idea that the class wasn't going to go on much further until someone volunteered an answer, someone blurted out "They'd probably start a fire."

> Model a way to deal with the perpetual problem of gaining students' attention at the beginning of class.

A few snickers floated through the room. "Well, sure. That's a possibility. Fire gives off both light and heat." Ms. Snyder continued, "Great grandpa could be nice and warm while he was reading. What are some other ways that could have been used to provide light?" She looked for the student who had snickered the loudest and posed the question again. "Well...I...uh....I don't know," the flustered boy gasped. "Oh sure you do...you just weren't quite ready for my question. Here, take a deep breath, then look at the ceiling for a minute while you collect your thoughts, and think of another possible light source." There was some fidgeting as many students now began to ponder the question and try to think of ways they might answer if called on. The wait seemed to go on forever; a glance at the clock was no help. It was as though the hands on the old dial face had slowed to a crawl, each second waiting until the

> Make the question personally relevant and show that you value the students' ideas.

last possible instant to pass as if reluctant to give up its grip on the present. "Why doesn't the teacher just give us the answer? She's supposed to know everything," one girl thought to herself. "Well, I know what I'll say if she calls on me. My mom has an old lamp in the basement that she said belonged to her mother. It burned whale fat...or something like that. What a silly answer that boy had, a fire would take too long to start compared with a lamp. Why didn't the teacher make fun of the answer?"

> Through modeling, demonstrate the safety of the class. This is not a place where answers will be ridiculed. It is a place where students will be responsible for participation, however long it takes.

She was still mulling over the situation when "A lamp" blurted out from somewhere. It was only a fraction of a second before she realized that she had offered the suggestion, almost without realizing it, her subconscious thoughts taking over her actions.

"Perfect timing...," Ms. Snyder thought as she began her carefully prepared discussion of the historical progression of light from oil lamps to electric bulbs, "Good answer. Yes, oil lamps were in very common use in the 1800s. Many different sources of oil were found, in fact..." Just then, the door squawked loudly in complaint as a student peeked through, handing over a message from the attendance office. Ms. Snyder started to feel frustration over the continual interruptions that occur during the day. Last year it had simply gotten out of control. This year would be different, she thought. She would attempt to take charge of her thought process and break the cycle of Disruption–Frustration–Anger–Disruption–More Frustration–Greater Anger.

This may even be the perfect example for Ms. Snyder to use with students when she begins the process of teaching them about their own psychological functioning and personal agency. The students can see how she takes control of the thought process to defuse the issue of interruptions, using an example that has relevance in this classroom. The students might even gain a feeling that the teacher is a "real" person.

The first week had passed quickly and, it seemed, successfully. Ms. Snyder's students had begun to understand and appreciate learning about their own thought process and how it determined behavior. The personal surveys that had been completed, like many before, surprised her with the amount of diversity in the class. Although some work still needed to be done as far as more carefully and realistically setting goals and objectives, it seemed that the students were beginning to take a very active part in determining their own project directions.

The class had gone especially well, even with the interruption of the unannounced fire drill. Ms. Snyder had been right in the middle of her dramatization of an 18th century character gathering firewood for the upcoming winter when the alarm had sounded. "No problem," she thought, as the class rose and started for the door. "I'll just announce as we go out that we are going out to help gather the fuel supplies. It might even be a nice break from the hot classroom. We could stay outside for a while and pretend we are in the forest trying to figure out a better way to provide heat energy for the cold months to come."

> Disruptions are particularly frustrating to teachers. Our own thought cycles progress as follows: Our thinking about disruption creates feelings of frustration. Our behavior becomes irritable. The cycle builds from disruption to disruption, the behavior becoming more and more obvious to students.

At the end of the period, after she had played the role of the research scientist looking for new ways to capture solar energy, she had everyone put away their supplies. "I thought we should take 15 minutes to discuss how well everyone seems to be doing in this class when others are relating how the projects are coming along. Your comments all seem to be really constructive and not in any way negative. I'm sure each of you has much better feelings about presenting in class without fear of others making fun of your efforts. Let's discuss some ways that can be used to tell presenters that we find their work interesting and that we each value the new knowledge they have provided."

In this example, the way in which Ms. Snyder's classroom has changed becomes apparent. The students have taken charge of much of the actual information gathering, managing, and reporting. The teacher has been spending less time preparing lesson plans on specific energy topics because that has, to a degree, become the responsibility of individual students, but she has had to spend more time facilitating the different student plans to complete projects.

Evaluating the projects has become especially time consuming because each one must be viewed in a way that is individually appropriate. Some suggestions for developing a positive, personalized assessment and reward system are as follows:

◻ Inform students at the planning stage what is expected when their projects are complete.

◻ Involve the students in an ongoing process of evaluation during project work.

◻ Use student conferences, when the normal class routine will not interfere with the process to allow time to discuss assessment.

◻ Use student self-evaluation, and show that you trust that students can be honest in evaluating their own work.

◻ Consider developing a system of peer grading.

◻ For projects that rely heavily on facilitation from teachers in other areas (such as industrial arts or physical education), consider involving those teachers in the grading process.

◻ Encourage students to take an active part in determining whether a traditional grade scale will be used for evaluation or if some other system of relating accomplishments to rewards would be more appropriate.

◻ Encourage parents or other community members to be a part of the reward establishment process.

1 What were some of the risks that Ms. Snyder was taking in the way that she managed her classroom? What were some of the risks she took in allowing students the freedom to pursue projects of individual interest?

2 Use the concept of the Thought Cycle to describe some ways that Ms. Snyder could get control over her fear of risk when allowing students so much freedom in their project selection. Use the Thought Cycle diagram to describe the thoughts, feelings, and behavior that she might exhibit.

3 What are some additional strategies that might be used to develop valid and meaningful systems of evaluation for student projects of great diversity?

CREATING A POSITIVE LEARNING CLIMATE

The final motivational strategy that we will discuss involves creating a positive climate of socioemotional support in which all students are individually and genuinely valued and respected. To do this, you need to know the personal qualities it takes to provide a supportive, trusting, and safe environment.

When individuals are placed in safe and positive environments and are in quality relationships with others, feelings of fear and insecurity are greatly reduced. For students at risk because of histories of school failure, negative attitudes toward themselves and school, or negative home or cultural backgrounds, feelings of insecurity and fears of taking risks are intense. These feelings are usually accompanied by distrustful, hostile, and aggressive feelings, feelings that can lead to withdrawn or acting out behaviors. When students don't understand their role in creating negative thoughts and biased perceptions of reality, or how feelings are influenced by their thinking, they are out of touch with their natural mental health and motivation. If caring adults create safe environments of trust and mutual respect, the insecure feelings of these students may be reduced and, like a cork rising to the surface, their natural good feelings, common sense, and motivation to learn and grow may resurface. It is in such an environment that students are in the best state of mind to learn. This is the best time to teach them about their own psychological functioning.

As a teacher, you understand that the source of motivation, self-esteem, and mental health comes from within and you know that a safe climate brings out this healthy core in students. You understand that if you react to or interact with students by judging, criticizing, or punishing, you may trigger or confirm students' negative thoughts and interpretations that are barriers to their expression of motivation and natural self-esteem. You understand that these negative behaviors will trigger feelings of insecurity in your students.

Activities to Create a Positive Learning Climate

Assessing One's Own Qualities as a Teacher

You need to be able to identify qualities within yourself that promote a positive learning climate as well as be able to assess the degree to which a positive climate exists within your classroom. A positive learning climate within the framework presented in this booklet is one of adult caring and interest, in which adults validate children's worth and significance and provide opportunities for relationship building. Youth can see models and experience mentoring relationships in a nurturing family atmosphere of mutual caring and support.

It is helpful to know how to assess your own personal qualities and the ways in which these can be used to foster the caring and interest in each child that is the cornerstone of a positive learning climate. It is also helpful to know how to consistently maintain the kinds of positive, motivational interactions with each student that help him or her see beyond negative or conditioned frames of reference. When you can assist students in this way, they can experience feelings of self-worth and a sense of personal control or agency. A climate of positive personal and social support helps both teachers and their students grow and learn successfully.

One good way to assess your own personal qualities, and to determine what qualities are needed to support a positive learning climate, is learning by example. Read the following examples and ask yourself, "Am I in this picture?"

EXAMPLE Mr. Able is very organized, disciplined, and structured. He likes to have his third-grade classroom look neat and orderly, with the desks lined up in rows, blackboards clean, and bulletin boards simple and well-arranged. He expects his students to sit quietly, not run or talk loudly, and obey all classroom rules. When rules are broken, students are sternly reprimanded and seated in a front row seat for the rest of the day. If you peeked into Mr. Able's classroom on any day, you'd find a well-disciplined, quiet atmosphere. His students seem serious and compliant.

Ms. Sonny's third-grade classroom could usually be described as loud and chaotic. Children are happily talking in small groups about today's topic or working on projects. The blackboard and bulletin boards are an array of student-generated projects and activities. There is an atmosphere of excitement and fun. Ms. Sonny can often be seen working individually with some of the students or walking around praising students for their activities.

Which classroom do you think has the best climate for learning? Obviously, the two classrooms described in these examples differ from one extreme to the other. What is important to note, however, is that certain qualities contribute to optimum learning and the enhancement of student motivation. Older views of motivation assumed that teachers could motivate behavior through external controls, rewards, or performance comparisons. More recent views reflect evidence that teachers who are less controlling and provide opportunities for student autonomy, initiative, and self-expression provide more effective environments for learning and motivation. In these autonomy-oriented environments characterized by active, interested, and constructive student–teacher interactions, students have been found to experience greater perceived competence, greater self-worth, and enhanced feelings of self-determination. In turn, their motivation and higher order learning are enhanced.

Let's see what that means in terms of teacher qualities. Here's a list of qualities identified in the research of Richard Ryan and Jerome Stiller.

Teachers who elicit students' intrinsic motivation are

◻ knowledgeable about each student's needs;

◻ interested in each student's development;

◻ consistent and firm regarding rules, limits, and resources supplied;

◻ democratic;

◻ encouraging;

◻ warm;

◻ positive about each student's ability to succeed; and

◻ respectful of all student performance attempts.

Other qualities identified in the research on teacher characteristics that are related to positive classroom climate include the following:

◻ being relaxed

◻ being able to have fun

◻ enjoying the work

◻ accentuating the positive

◻ setting consistent limits

◻ disciplining without putting students down

◻ encouraging students to take risks

◻ not expecting perfection

◻ having a sense of humor

◻ dealing with discipline as privately as possible

◻ remembering that students are not bad or deficient, just insecure

◻ knowing how to forgive and forget

◻ never giving up

All of these qualities convey a feeling of respect and caring. They are the basis of quality student–teacher relationships.

Assessing Classroom Climate

A second attribute that can help you establish a positive climate for learning in your classroom is the ability to assess that climate. The following dimensions are important in evaluating the climate in your classroom:

◻ **A safe and orderly environment:** Students are respected as individuals and for their cultural differences; rules and procedures are well-defined and clearly communicated.

◻ **Collaborative decision making:** Both teachers and students are involved in establishing goals, rules, and operating procedures so there is a sense of shared responsibility and of collegiality.

◻ **High expectations for all students:** The focus is on student learning and student acceptance of responsibility; all students are expected to be successful in reaching learning goals.

◻ **Encouragement of student initiative:** The teacher provides opportunities for student-generated activities and other responsibilities by giving students appropriate levels of choice (e.g., choosing topics of interest, choosing how they want to demonstrate what they've learned).

□ **Acceptance of many viewpoints and solutions to problems:** The teacher isn't always the final authority but shares expertise with students; tolerance for unique opinions and the relativity of knowledge on complex issues is acknowledged and modeled.

□ **Feelings and ideas are valued:** The diverse feelings and ideas offered by students are accepted and valued.

A number of other dimensions have been used by researchers to look at classroom climate. Typically these have involved the degree to which students perceive the classroom to have the following positive characteristics, and to lack the following negative characteristics:

Positive Climate Indicators

cohesion—students know, help, and are friendly toward each other

diversity—different student interests are encouraged

formality—behavior is guided by formal rules

cooperation—emphasis is on students cooperating with one another

satisfaction—students enjoy class work

concern—teachers are sensitive to social and emotional needs of individual students

democracy—students share in decision making

goal direction—class goals are clear

Negative Climate Indicators

favoritism—the teacher treats some students more favorably than others

difficulty—class work is at an inappropriate level of difficulty for students

friction—tension and quarreling are regular occurrences among students

competition—emphasis is on students competing with one another

social control—teachers impose their expectations in an authoritative way and exercise power without regard for student needs

SUMMARY

In Goal 4, we have focused on several strategies that help establish the kind of classroom climate in which students' natural motivation to learn can emerge. These strategies are (a) finding ways to help students take increasing responsibility for their own learning and meeting the need for self-determination through student choice and control; (b) helping students become academic risk takers through modeling, skill training, and self-assessment strategies; and (c) understanding yourself and how these qualities relate to establishing a positive climate for learning.

In the final analysis, the most important ingredients for reaching hard to motivate students are a commitment to the growth of each learner and a commitment to personal growth. Your students will feel and respond to these qualities, combined with your subject matter expertise and your expertise in teaching strategies. When they feel comfortable, secure, and genuinely respected and cared about, and when they have been encouraged to see their own potential to learn, even the most difficult students can be reached and can once again experience the motivation to learn.

Teachers who are best at reaching the most difficult to reach youth are those who are consistently upbeat and unafraid, and have a consistent empathic regard for their students. The research has consistently shown that students from home, community, or peer group environments that place them at risk need experiences with adults who exemplify the characteristics of responsibility, maturity, and positive human relationships, and who establish an atmosphere of mutual caring and support. Once implemented, the tools and tips presented here can further enhance students' abilities to understand their personal agency in taking responsibility for their own learning and self-development.

One final tip: It is critical that you maintain your own level of mental health and positive functioning. If you are functioning under a great deal of stress, suffering from burnout, or do not feel comfortable dealing with hard to motivate students, you will find it difficult to maintain the types of positive qualities in your interactions with these students that are necessary to bring out their healthier levels of functioning. The better you understand the way your thinking can cause negative feelings (like stress), as well as see how this operates in high-risk students, the easier it will become for you to maintain your poise and respect for youth. In this healthier state of mind, you will find it easier to help hard to motivate youth to function in more positive states of mind. In these states of mind, the students' natural motivation will surface, and their mental health will return. The process is reciprocal.

1 | Describe the five teacher functions in the role of motivator.

2 | Why is it important to teach students about their psychological functioning before they proceed to develop individual student projects?

3 | Draw a Thought Cycle to depict the Thought–Feeling–Behavior cycle of a teacher in a situation in which he or she might feel professionally threatened by a student who becomes an expert in a specific area and consequently more knowledgeable about a topic than the teacher. How can the teacher use his or her knowledge of the thought process to break the cycle and be comfortable in the situation described?

4 | What elements lead to the creation of a positive climate in the classroom? What signs would you look for in students that would indicate they are working in such a climate?

ANSWERS TO QUESTIONS

1 The five teacher functions are

a. Teach students about their psychological functioning and their personal agency in creating and directing thoughts that impact motivation and learning.

b. Help students value themselves, the learning process, and specific learning activities.

c. Create opportunities for students' natural tendencies to learn, grow, and take responsibility for their own learning.

d. Encourage academic risk taking to offset potentially negative consequences of the schooling experience such as boredom, fear of failure, and withdrawal.

e. Create a positive climate of personal and social support in which all students are individually and genuinely valued and respected.

2 By understanding and being aware of the ways beliefs and feelings are related in their own thought cycle, students can become aware of how their behavior is often artificially controlled. By recognizing that separate realities often distort their view of the learning environment, students can alter their views and grow to value the learning process and specific learning activities.

3 The diagrams may vary; however, responses about the use of the diagram should indicate that the teacher now understands that his or her behavior, manifested in the form of fear, is a result of the belief and thought that teachers are supposed to have all of the answers. Once the teacher recognizes the fallacy of the teacher as "knower of all things," he or she can break the cycle at the thought stage and eliminate the fear.

4 **a.** These can include that limits are consistent, students are disciplined in ways that do not put them down, students are encouraged to take risks, discipline is dealt with privately, and teachers and students both know how to forgive and forget.

b. Students are relaxed, have fun, are working on tasks without teacher intervention, and do not give up on difficult tasks.

1 List those qualities discussed here (and some of your own, if you like) that you think you could use to establish a positive climate for learning in your classroom.

2 Review the teacher qualities and dimensions of classroom climate listed in the past few pages. Use these to construct your personal "Classroom Climate Inventory."

3 Look back at the examples of Sasha and Derrin at the beginning of this booklet. Read what you wrote about how to motivate these students. Would you suggest different approaches or strategies now? Write down any insights or changes in how you might deal with these two students.

With Sasha, I would:

With Derrin, I would:

Checking Back

With Sasha and Derrin

Based on the philosophy and strategies presented in this book for motivating hard to reach students, examples of how a teacher might work with Sasha and Derrin are presented below.

SASHA

Sasha's teacher considers Sasha's withdrawn behavior and, once again, thinks through the reasons for it. The teacher sees that Sasha is struggling with her reading and that other children in the class are making fun of her. The teacher also reflects on her own feelings of impatience and frustration with Sasha and realizes that whether she means to or not, she probably communicates these feelings to Sasha. The teacher begins to understand that Sasha probably feels like a failure, and that this must be very painful to her. Now that she understands Sasha's point of view, the teacher can begin to explore strategies for addressing Sasha's need to feel competent.

Sasha's teacher wants to help her work on improving her skills in a way that will feel comfortable, non-threatening, and personally supportive to Sasha. Her goal is to help Sasha experience a sense of mastery in reading and a sense of acceptance by other students. In addition, her teacher recognizes the value of accomplishing this goal in a way that actively involves Sasha in decisions and, therefore, has personal meaning and relevance for Sasha.

Given this perspective, there are many things that Sasha's teacher could do. For example, the teacher might begin planning how she will talk to Sasha about things Sasha really likes to do and things she would like to learn about. Using this information, the teacher plans to suggest different ways that Sasha could learn about these things by reading, and she also plans to work with Sasha to choose reading activities. In order to address some of Sasha's social needs, the teacher begins planning ways she will involve the children in cooperative learning groups of mixed reading ability. In addition, she sees that she will need to be sure that she provides personal support and encouragement to Sasha in order to help her develop her unique talents and abilities.

DERRIN

Derrin's teachers are part of an eighth-grade team at his middle school. The team begins to think about Derrin's absences and disruptive behavior. They see that Derrin has personal and family difficulties that contribute to his behavior. Together, they reflect on their responses to Derrin and how their own feelings of concern and frustration about not knowing how they can reach him may in fact be pushing him away. They begin to realize how tough it must be for Derrin to continually have to re-enter school and connect with people. The teachers begin to understand that Derrin's need to feel that he belongs is not being met and that this prevents him from becoming engaged and involved in school.

Because Derrin has very few friends in the school, and his home life offers little in terms of a supportive adult relationship, the teachers agree that they want to help him develop the skills he needs for making friends and for getting involved in the school's social activities. The team's goal is to help Derrin feel that he has some positive relationships that he can rely on with people who care about and respect him. The teachers realize that Derrin's family situation and current interests must be acknowledged and respected. In this way, they plan to build a foundation of trust with Derrin that can be used as a bridge to help him explore different options for meeting his needs. They understand that when they help him become more involved in meeting his social needs, and when he feels respected and cared about, he will be more open to becoming engaged in school and in learning.

Derrin's team of teachers discuss a range of options for approaching and winning Derrin's trust. They also look at the types of school activities and special interest clubs in which Derrin might want to become involved. One of the teachers proposes starting an after-school club for students who could benefit from positive activities. It could be a place where students, with support from teachers and even adults from the community, could go to enjoy themselves, pursue their interests with adult mentors, and build on and gain basic life and social skills. The team feels this is a good idea and that Derrin might even want to help plan such a club. It would be a good opportunity for him to work with his teacher team on a nonacademic project, while at the same time learning to trust others and learning how to design a program that can meet his and other students' needs. Bringing Derrin and other students into the planning process is also considered an empowerment strategy that would help at-risk students feel they have some control over the ways their needs are met within the context of school.

final review

This book has provided a perspective on the nature of motivation to learn and how it can be enhanced in hard to motivate students. The information and suggestions are based on current research and theory from a perspective that views motivation to learn as inherent in all individuals and as a natural state to be elicited from students rather than established. In eliciting student motivation to learn, it is important that teachers recognize the following:

□ An individual's motivation is based on that person's previously learned beliefs about his or her worth and abilities.

□ An individual will establish expectations of success or failure and will develop either positive or negative feelings about learning based on learned beliefs.

□ Both internal (e.g., beliefs, expectations, and goals) and external (e.g., rewards, support, and approval from others) factors play important roles in defining the nature of motivation and how to enhance its effect.

□ At higher levels of the thought process, students have the ability to understand the relationship between their system of beliefs and their natural tendency to be self-motivated.

□ Individuals are often unaware of their role in constructing thoughts and personal realities.

□ Intrinsic motivation to learn is part of a naturally existing core of positive mental health available to everyone.

In examining what this view of the nature of motivation implies for the role of the teacher as motivator, changing notions about this role were discussed. Because learning is now understood as an active process in which students are responsible for their own progress and accomplishments, the teacher's primary role is to facilitate the learning process rather than to present information.

Five important strategies for teachers to use in helping students to be self-motivated were identified:

1. teaching students about their psychological functioning and their personal agency in creating and directing thoughts that impact motivation and learning;

2. helping students value themselves, the learning process, and specific learning activities;

3. creating opportunities for students to demonstrate their natural tendencies to learn, grow, and take responsibility for their own learning;

4. encouraging academic risk taking to offset potentially negative consequences of the schooling experience such as boredom, fear of failure, and withdrawal; and

5. creating a positive climate of personal and social support in which all students are individually and genuinely valued and respected.

As a first step in putting these roles into practice, we elaborated on some of the basic concepts and principles related to each of the strategies. Information was provided on (a) helping students and teachers understand and bypass or override negative thoughts and feelings; (b) helping teachers personally get to know each student while also helping students define their interests and goals; (c) helping teachers structure their teaching approach to encourage student choice and increased student responsibility for learning; (d) helping students develop skills to become academic risk takers; and (e) helping teachers understand the personal qualities it takes to provide a supportive, trusting, and safe environment and to assess their own classroom climate.

Suggestions were then provided for classroom strategies and activities that can be used to enhance motivation for all students, particularly hard to motivate students. These suggestions were provided to stimulate the teachers' creativity in designing particular strategies and activities to meet the needs of their unique classrooms and students. We hope you are left with these thoughts: To truly elicit each student's natural motivation to learn, teachers need to provide quality relationships and environments of mutual caring and support. Maintaining their own mental health is critical to bringing out healthier levels of functioning in students. An understanding of the principles and strategies presented in this book can help you understand your own mental health and motivation in addition to helping you uncover it in your students.

In this exciting and often frustrating era of major school reform, and in the midst of major challenges brought on by changing student populations and needs, it will take time to implement the strategies suggested in this book. Try a few things with a few students. See what happens. If you find the strategies helpful, you will find a way to use them more and more. Your successes can then be a model for your colleagues.

glossary

adaptive belief patterns—Individuals' beliefs that they can successfully accomplish learning goals and that their self-worth is not conditional on external factors (e.g., the opinions of others or the ability to perform relative to others).

agency—An inherent tendency of the self to originate behavior; inherent capacity for self-determination and personal control of thoughts, feelings, and behavior.

autonomy—Self-regulation or an individual's experience of volition, self-expression, initiative, or self-determination.

behavior—Actions that result from individuals' prior beliefs, and the manner in which thoughts are processed in response to external situations; a reaction to specific thoughts and feelings in a given situation.

cognition—Intellectual capabilities, including thinking, information processing, memory, and factual knowledge; contrasted with affect (feelings, emotions) and metacognition (higher order thinking capabilities).

conditioning—A process of acquiring information that is relatively automatic; habitual responses learned through relatively unconscious processes.

dysfunctional—Learned patterns of thinking, feeling, and behaving that are unhealthy and do not promote positive learning and self-development; patterns that operate outside of an individual's awareness of his or her innate core of mental health.

elicit—Draw out or bring about; an enhancement of naturally occurring capacities; contrasted with *establish* as the action for reaching students' natural motivation.

extrinsic—External or outside of the individual; used to refer to the external factors that play a role in influencing individuals' motivation to learn.

facilitation—Comprehensive guidance and management that does not involve taking the primary responsibility for an outcome; literally, to make easier, as in a teacher's role in facilitating student motivation to learn.

feeling—The emotion that results from specific thoughts and beliefs; leads to behavior or specific reactions to the thoughts and beliefs.

innate—Inherent or existing as a naturally occurring capacity or function of the individual.

intrinsic—Internal or inherent in the individual; used to refer to the naturally occurring motivation to learn in individuals.

metacognition—Capacity for higher order thinking about one's thinking; an executive level of control that includes processes such as self-monitoring, self-evaluation, and planning; capacity that leads to the self-awareness of one's agency or personal control over thoughts, feelings, and behavior.

model, modeling—To set an example; providing observable demonstrations of personal qualities, skills, and other attributes that can be emulated.

motivation—A natural capacity and tendency within individuals to learn and grow in positive ways; aimed at achieving personal goals.

perception—Awareness or consciousness of internal and external factors affecting one's functioning or experience; can be influenced by one's beliefs and form a filter for processing information and experiencing reality.

psychological functioning—Levels of mental operation that reflect individuals' awareness of principles of thought, consciousness, and inherent capacities for mental health.

reciprocal—Two-way influence or interaction; used to refer to the impact on the teacher and student alike.

self-actualization—State or level of psychological functioning in which individuals are operating from a higher level of understanding of their personal agency and innate capacity for mental health (including wisdom, insight, and creativity).

self-esteem—Positive regard for oneself; a feeling, perception, or judgment of positive self-worth; an inherent capacity for unconditional feelings of worth and well-being.

separate realities—Individually constructed systems of beliefs that serve to personalize one's experience of life; they are unique to each individual due to operation of the thought cycle and individuals' unique perceptual filters.

skill—An acquired cognitive or metacognitive competency that develops with training and/or practice.

socioemotional support—Actions or systems that meet individual emotional and social needs (e.g., needs to be valued, seen as worthy and significant, cared about, respected); provided in an environment characterized by quality relationships of mutual respect, caring, and concern.

thought—Process by which an individual constructs and uses beliefs to interpret current experience; creates feelings and behavior and is subject to individual control and choice.

will—An innate or self-actualized state of motivation; an internal state of well-being in which individuals are in touch with their natural self-esteem, common sense, and intrinsic motivation to learn.

ABOUT THE AUTHORS

Barbara L. McCombs is the Director of the Motivation and Human Development Team at the Mid-continent Regional Educational Laboratory in Aurora, Colorado. She has a PhD in Educational Psychology from Florida State University. She has nearly 20 years of experience in research and development of motivational interventions for students, teachers, and parents. Her particular area of expertise is empowerment strategies that enhance the intrinsic motivation and self-regulated learning skills of individuals.

James E. Pope is a middle school science teacher for Aurora public schools and works at West Middle School teaching science and mathematics. He has a BS degree in engineering physics from the Colorado School of Mines and an MA in secondary education from the University of Colorado at Denver. He has been teaching for 7 years and is particularly interested in using technology to enhance interdisciplinary instruction. His expertise is developing personal responsibility and motivation in at-risk students.